The Enchantment
of the Middle Ages

PARALLAX RE-VISIONS OF CULTURE
AND SOCIETY

Stephen G. Nichols, Gerald Prince, and Wendy Steiner
SERIES EDITORS

The Enchantment
of the Middle Ages

Michel Zink

TRANSLATED BY
Jane Marie Todd

The Johns Hopkins University Press
Baltimore and London

Originally published as *Le Moyen Age et ses chansons, ou un Passé en trompe-l'oeil,* © Éditions de Fallois, 1996

On behalf of the editors of Parallax, the Johns Hopkins
University Press wishes to thank the Florence Gould
Foundation for its support of the translation of this volume.

The Johns Hopkins University Press
2715 North Charles Street
Baltimore, Maryland 21218-4319
The Johns Hopkins Press Ltd., London

Library of Congress Cataloging-in-Publication Data will
be found at the end of this book.
A catalog record for this book is available from the
British Library.

ISBN 0-8018-5818-6

Contents

■ Foreword

America has no institution like the Collège de France. Founded at the height of the Renaissance by François I in 1530, it was conceived as a means of assuring the continued preeminence of French thought on the European—then world—scene. The king's advisors conceived the Collège as an independent research institution enabling the best minds in France to devote full time to their disciplines, which they then would interpret to the public.

To this day, those elected to the Collège do not teach in the usual academic sense of the term. Instead, as François I intended, they ponder deeply the meaning of knowledge in their respective fields and then explain their findings to the public at large. This means that they have simultaneously to create new frontiers in their fields *and* to expound their findings not to a specialized audience but to lay people who come to hear their weekly lectures in surprisingly large numbers. Only a handful of the most intelligent and lively minds in France reach the Collège—people like Roland Barthes, Maurice Merleau-Ponty, Michel Foucault, Pierre Bourdieu—and once there, they exert a powerful influence on the nature of the work being done in their discipline. Indeed, without them, their field might well not be studied at the Collège, for in a real sense, it is the person, not the subject, who is elected. When a professor retires from his or her chair, it may be filled by a specialist in a very different domain of knowledge.

Medieval French had not been represented for a generation when Michel Zink was elected to the Collège in 1994. It was the best thing that could have happened to the discipline, for Michel Zink has spearheaded a rally for medieval French studies in France sparked by his *oeuvre*, on the one hand, and, on the other, by his media talent—

he regularly appears on radio, for example—not to mention his useful bilingual editions of a growing range of medieval French works published in his Lettres Gothiques series at Livre de Poche. But even beyond his publications, he has represented, perhaps more than anyone else, medieval French literature on the global scene thanks to lectures delivered literally all over the world. Where Zink has been, medieval French studies do not languish.

Beginning with the United States. Almost from the start of his career, Michel Zink has traveled the length and breadth of North America, speaking at well-known and lesser-known colleges and universities with the same charm, ever displaying his special blend of literary acumen and verve. He has been a visiting professor at Berkeley, Yale, Penn, Dartmouth, and Johns Hopkins and a regularly invited speaker at a number of universities and conferences in the United States and Canada, where he is always a great favorite. Not surprisingly, universities on both coasts tried to hire him over the years.

Though a virtuoso, Michel Zink is not a one-man band. He possesses a talent for rallying scholars to his cause. Even before his elevation to the Collège de France, he had established himself as an international leader. In his Lettres Gothiques series, for example, Zink enlists scholars from all over Europe and North America as editors and translators. In consequence, the series offers bilingual editions of an astonishing number of Old and Middle French texts, including some that have not been available for generations (if ever). Similarly, he regularly invites foreign scholars who have distinguished themselves in some aspect of the seminar topic to speak at the Collège. In this way, Michel Zink leverages his post at the Collège de France to create an international focus for medieval French studies. One could hardly imagine a more fitting postmodern means for realizing François I's aspirations.

Publications, lots of them, and of the highest quality, mark those who aspire to the Collège. So it is no surprise to find that Michel Zink has published some twenty-two books in all, twelve of them wholly authored by him. They range from high-energy literary criticism, like his study of poetic subjectivity, to coauthored manuals and

handbooks of Old French literature which most of us use at least
once a day. His early studies of the pastourelle and his work on sermon literature in Old French quickly established Zink as an innova-
tive thinker determined to push the boundaries of the discipline to
include material frequently overlooked or underestimated. His virtuosity in reading lyric poetry expanded to the romance with the publication of his book on Jean Renart's *Romance of the Rose*, a fascinat-
ing precursor to Guillaume de Lorris's more famous allegory of the
same name.

Jean Renart's romance had been largely neglected when Zink re-
minded readers that this was in a real sense the first "experimental"
novel, experimental in defining a new form for romance by the expedient of explicitly "quoting" lyric poetry in a setting of "straight" narrative, and experimental in showing that the romance was, after all, a
courtly diversion, like the dances it featured, as well as an esthetic
construction on the same plane as the elaborately decorated materials in the gowns worn by the women of the court. Experimental also
in making the courtly woman's body a text or ground for erotic spec-
ulation (the plot turns on a birthmark shaped like a red rose on the
heroine's thigh).

Readers learn just how subtly medieval authors used ordinary language to make new meaning thanks to Zink's sensitivity in elucidat-
ing poetic style. He can convey hitherto unrecognized language
games in a work by the simple expedient of adapting an example for
his titles. Take, for example, this engaging study: *Roman rose et rose
rouge*. The title is untranslatable precisely because it conveys a whole
set of connotations keyed to the way the work juxtaposes language
and the body. A literal rendering, *Rose romance and red rose*, makes no
sense unless one realizes that "rose" has the connotation of "pink" as
well as "rose" and the "rose rouge" refers to the birthmark on the
heroine's thigh, as well as the esthetic "coloring" of the text, and the
rose that is both pink and a flower also possesses an erotic connotation. Zink's title—and book—capture all this, but they also make
modern readers aware that the true virtuosity belongs to Jean Renart.

We can now glimpse just how much Zink's early books set him

apart as a scholar with a keen sense of literary art. Their range also made it clear that he intended nothing less than to tackle the full range of Old French literature. Not for him the safety of a narrow niche. He could do so with confidence because he is an extraordinary reader of texts. Like Vladimir Nabokov, who used to urge undergraduates in his European literature course at Cornell University to "caress the details," Michel Zink shows that literature lives through its parts—be it the "pop" hits of the early-twelfth-century lyric intercalated in Jean Renart's *Romance of the Rose* or the subtle variations of the use of the first person in lyric and romance which he traces with something akin to philosophical precision in his great work on literary subjectivity in medieval French literature.

The present book occupies a special place in Zink's *oeuvre*, however. It will certainly force us, as his books usually do, to revise our sense of the relationship of Old French lyric poetry to the past that it so confidently appeals to. And yet, this book is about so much more than the history of medieval lyric—however complex that may be in itself. It is a book that defends and illustrates the discipline of medieval literature itself. It could be nothing else, motivated as it is by the event that occasioned it: Michel Zink's election to the Collège de France. Tradition requires the newly elected chair holders to give an inaugural lecture that will be followed by their first seminar. The lecture, and, by implication, the course, must somehow speak to the importance of the subject or discipline represented by the chair holder. Together, they announce to the world at large why it matters that a Michel Zink or a Claude Lévi-Strauss or a Georges Duby or a Michel Foucault will henceforth be lecturing on their subject at the Collège de France and why it is that French thinkers have something rather special to say, something that the rest of us might profit by hearing.

In consequence, inaugural lessons and courses at the Collège function as indexes of the state of a discipline at a given moment in time. Several recent studies that come to mind review at length the inaugural lessons of the first chairs of medieval French studies, Paulin Paris, in 1854—Napoleon III established the Chair of Medieval French Language and Literature specifically for him in 1853—and that of his son, Gaston, in 1870. Michel Zink pays genuine homage to this tradition and to the modern founders of the discipline of medieval studies in his inauguration. On the one hand his subject: the medieval French lyric, but that topic foregrounds, as a second argument, the theories of the founders of the discipline whom Zink generously recognizes throughout the book. Yet in the best tradition of such events, he replays the songs of his illustrious predecessors the better to show how his own views diverge from theirs.

It's a delicate game. One needs on the one hand to pay homage to the genius of the founders, to concede that twelfth-century topos that one is a dwarf standing on the shoulders of giants. At the same time, one has also to demonstrate that one may fairly lay claim to that status oneself lest the prestige of the institution suffer. Election to the Collège does not confer greatness, after all; it recognizes it. The inaugural lesson and subsequent course must reveal to the world the quality of the inductee. The occasion requires, then, something like an exhibition of the inductee's ability to rethink his discipline, especially with respect to predecessors.

That is why lyric poetry does not inhabit this work innocently. It recognizes a central preoccupation of the Paris, père et fils; announces a powerful revisionist hypothesis of Zink's own—indeed, this book launches one of the most original theses on medieval French lyric poetry in recent memory—and, finally, stands as a kind of metaphor for medieval literature in general as it has tended to be studied.

For Paulin and Gaston Paris, though for different reasons, medieval lyric poetry was the most important of the literary genres. They believed that literature organized itself inevitably according to types that then formed a hierarchy with lyric poetry squarely at the top. Why? Because, for Paulin Paris, lyric poetry was the most ancient form of literary expression in France. It represented the lyric childhood of the people and was, accordingly, a spontaneous testimony of the origins of French culture. Gaston found his father's romanticism embarrassing. For him, the greatness of Old French lyric must be sought in its aristocratic and learned nature, qualities that come to be denoted by the term "courtly." Indeed, it was Gaston

Paris who invented the term "courtly love" in part for this purpose. Gaston did not altogether reject his father's argument about the pastness of lyric poetry, however. He conceded that it yields vestiges of popular culture: Beneath its courtly form one might still hear the voice of the people.

Michel Zink does not expose these theories and those of successor incumbents to the chair of medieval literature—Joseph Bédier, Mario Roques, Félix Lecoy (Zink is the sixth in line of succession since its founding in 1853)—in order to show how wrong they were. On the contrary, he reviews them by way of reminding us just how crucial a role they have played in setting the bounds of the discipline over the last 150 years. He shows—and here we see how lyric functions as an index for medieval literature generally—that even though Bédier, Gaston Paris's student and great successor, worked with narrative, rather than lyric genres (fabliau, lay, and epic), his preoccupation with the origins of epic simply displaced Gaston Paris's interest in the courtly origin and venue of lyric to the sanctuary of the pilgrimage routes where Bédier situated the rationale for the epic which he summed up in his famous dictum: *Au commencement fut la route, la route jalonnée de sanctuaires* [In the beginning was the pilgrim road bordered by saints' churches]. In short, if Bédier shifted his attention from courtly to religious settings, from lyric to epic, the moves still owed much to the formulations of Paulin and Gaston Paris. One could continue to trace the affinities even in the midst of differences among Zink's predecessors at the Collège. His point, however, does not lie there.

He takes pains to show the massive coherence of their work—as well as its overwhelming influence on medieval French studies—in order to show how deeply each was committed to the idea of the pastness of medieval literature. Its value, for them, lay precisely in their unshakable belief that in the commitment of medieval French literature to demonstrating the past, a prehistory before written records, lay a guarantee of the enduring wholeness of France, the unity of its language and its culture. And it was just those qualities that the chair of medieval language and literature had been founded to demonstrate. Let us not forget that 1853, the beginning of the Second Empire, was not uncoincidentally a high point in the evolution of French nationalism.

Michel Zink's bombshell consists quite simply in asking whether the pastness of medieval French literature might not, like the red rose of Jean Renart's romance, be a consequence of its artifice. The original French title of this book was projected as "Leurres du passé," a pun on *leurre* (trap) and *l'heure* (hour) in the sense of time (past). Scholars have focused on the origins of medieval French literature, on its obsession with the past, precisely because it encouraged them to do so. They concluded, in a sense, that because they were concerned with bridging the trauma of the Revolution and establishing a unified tradition of continuity in French language and literature, and because they believed in the power of literature to do both of these things, their subject must bear them out, proving their case beyond a reasonable doubt.

Zink refuses to dismiss the work of his predecessors simply because, in a sense, they were duped by their texts. Instead, his study begins where other scholars might have triumphantly thought to end, having trumped the founders. In a wonderful aphorism, he observes: "The best reason to continue to teach medieval literature as we have been doing for over 150 years now is to contemplate the possibility that its object doesn't exist." I will leave readers the pleasure of discovering for themselves the magic that Michel Zink finds to put in its place.

Stephen G. Nichols
The Johns Hopkins University

Prefatory Note

This little book contains the inaugural lecture for
the chair of medieval French literature at the Collège de France, delivered 24 March 1995, and the course that followed in May of the
same year. The reader will therefore not be surprised to find that the
more elevated tone of the inaugural lecture is followed by the infor-
mal remarks and meandering of a course, which is reproduced here
more or less as it was delivered.

*The Enchantment
of the Middle Ages*

Inaugural Lecture

Deep forests, enchanted castles, monsters, maidens in distress, stout-hearted heroes, boundless love: The literature of the Middle Ages has the power to entrance the imaginations of children and adolescents. But can it do more than that? And in fact, does that power of enchantment still work? Anatole France claimed that his pretty little neighbor preferred "scientific novels," in which she could read a description of the cuttlefish, *Sepia officinalis,* to the loves of Abeille des Clarides and Georges de Blanchelande and the magnanimity of the king of dwarves.[1] Of course, *Abeille,* whose prologue I invoke here, is not truly a story from the Middle Ages. Of course, this prologue surrenders to an accommodating simplicity. And of course, the author's notion of both medieval legends and positive science is very dated. But all the same, if the only thrilling novels that exist deal with the progress of the natural sciences, what remains for us, we who claim to bring vanished dreams back to life? If that is the case, then our colleagues, the true scientists, have indeed taken everything from us, and it is only their excessive generosity or indulgence that leads them to make a place for us among them.

That place at least has age in its favor. A chair of French language and literature of the Middle Ages was created at the Collège de

France for Paulin Paris in 1853. It kept that name when it passed to his son, Gaston Paris, then to Joseph Bédier, and, having received the name of chair in the history of French vocabulary for Mario Roques, recovered its original name for M. Félix Lecoy. In addition, from 1876 to 1906 the chair of languages and literatures of southern Europe, which M. Harald Weinrich now holds, was occupied by Paul Meyer, whose work focused primarily on French and Occitan philology. Finally, between 1925 and 1954 a chair of Latin literature of the Middle Ages existed, held by Edmond Faral. Not to mention the preponderant place of medieval studies in the activities associated with the chair of Celtic languages and literature, occupied by Henry d'Arbois de Jubainville from 1882 to 1930, then by Joseph Loth, and with the chair of languages and literature of Germanic origin, particularly between 1934 and 1956, under the impetus of Ernest Tonnelat and Fernand Mossé. Then there was the interest manifested in literature by medievalists from other disciplines, such as Etienne Gilson, or by those who distinguished the teaching of medieval history, in particular M. Georges Duby and now M. Pierre Toubert. In a word, to return to and remain with the discipline of French, Occitan, and Latin, the philology and literature of the Middle Ages were taught without interruption at the Collège de France from 1853 to 1974 and sometimes simultaneously in several posts.

And by such masters! As Francesco Novati observed, Gaston Paris, forefather of our studies, was able to make the most complex and arid subject matter appealing and clear.[2] His alter ego and conscience, the severe Paul Meyer, "mark[ed] each error with a sharp fingernail," as Anatole France—again—describes him through the words of his character Sylvestre Bonnard.[3] Finding strength in his rigor, Meyer also brought a decisive expertise to his testimony on behalf of Alfred Dreyfus, an expertise to which Proust pays a magnificent homage in *Jean Santeuil*.[4] Then there was the brilliant, entrancing, subtle Bédier, whose adaptation of *Tristan et Iseut* (Tristram and Isolde), done half in jest, stands as one of the prominent literary works of the century that was then coming to a close.[5] There was Edmond Faral, who was an administrator of this place, and M. Lecoy, of an inexhaustible erudition, ironic and kind, who taught us to put all we have into what we are doing but without exaggerating its importance to ourselves, for therein lies elegance and reason. Yes, the teaching of the literatures of medieval France, which is being reborn today, can lay claim to a long tradition, an overwhelming tradition if we think of the quality of all those who devoted themselves to it in the past.

The length of a tradition, of course, would not in itself be a reason to preserve or restore that teaching if tradition did not have something to do with the object itself. All the associations between the past and literature, all the signs that there is an essential link between the notion of literature and a feeling for the past, crystallize in medieval letters. The curiosity awakened by the literature of the Middle Ages, beginning with its rediscovery at the dawn of romanticism, presupposes such associations. The forms of that literature itself conceal such signs. They invite us to embrace in a single glance the interest the modern age shows in the medieval past and the signs of the past with which medieval writers marked their own literature. Even more, they invite us to seek in the relation with the past a criterion for the very definition of literature. That task is particularly necessary in the case of an age when the word *literature* was not yet used in its modern sense and in which the very existence of the corresponding notion is not assured. The best reason to pursue this 150-year-old course of study is that its object may not exist.

Let us pretend, however, that it does exist. We have the right to do so. Of course, the word *litteratura* designated either grammar or commentary on the author's works with the knowledge it procured, but not the set of works themselves. Of course, the vernacular languages did not possess any generic term for literary activity or literary works. But in the Middle Ages, there was nonetheless an awareness of such an activity and of a corpus of works. In the case of Latin, this was indicated by the word *litterae*, meaning literary culture, by the continual reflection on the nature and legitimacy of belles-lettres, by the permanence of a canon of authors from Antiquity, and by the systematic practice of borrowings and imitation. In the case of productions in the vernacular, in which the situation is more ambiguous, a set of poems, also canonical in its way, fairly early on constituted the obligatory repertoire of the jongleurs.[6] At the beginning of *Cligès*, Chrétien de Troyes enumerates his earlier works, combining translations of Ovid and Breton romances, as if in his eyes the unity of the writing prevailed over the disparateness of the subject matter.[7] The troubadours continually responded to one another and cited one another, marking by the play of the intertext the closed and identifiable contours of a realm of poetry.[8] The systematic adaptations or translations of chansons de geste and of French romances into German or Norse in the thirteenth century, and their later constant circulation and reworking, also suggest a synthetic vision of literary production.[9]

If we grant that medieval literature exists, its most striking character with respect to European literature as a whole is that it constitutes that literature's beginning. An absolute beginning, in a certain way, when it finds expression in the Romance languages, which had just come into being. A beginning that seems to suppose at every moment an inaccessible prehistory in the form of oral productions or a mythical substratum whose traces or wreckage we believe we can discern. A beginning that is not a beginning, because that literature is the heir to classical letters—though it does not ensure their continuity—because it makes the imitation of those letters one of its founding principles, and because Latin occupies a vital and privileged place within it. That birth and that inheritance are the traits that first held people's attention: a new literature in new languages; a literature schooled in Latin letters, written partly in Latin, but whose irreducible originality was never so noticeable as when it claimed to reproduce classical models.

What a discovery! Here was something truly new! And even more than one might think. The term "Middle Ages" defines the age not in itself but negatively or in silhouette, in relation to the age that preceded and the age that followed; even this term, however, which appeared in the eighteenth century, is significant in its historical representation of arts and letters, especially since it replaced expressions such as "barbarous times" or "dark ages," which expressed a value judgment. Antiquity could serve as a model for French and European classicism, as long as the hypothesis of a permanence of forms of wit and taste lasted. As soon as attention was drawn to the changes that affect forms, as soon as people began to deduce from these forms a reflection on aesthetics and history, the Middle Ages attracted interest.

It is no accident that the first person to truly conceive of the Middle Ages within a philosophy of history and an aesthetics was Hegel. Before him, Vico had viewed the poetic imagination as the mark of childhood, the childhood of civilizations as well as individuals; and Herder, in his confused and sometimes contradictory fashion, had conferred considerable importance on the poetry of the Middle Ages for the linguistic, artistic, and national development of European peoples.[10] He thus lent theoretical support to the attraction for ancient poetic traditions that, since Percy and Macpherson, had manifested itself throughout Europe.[11] Everything is contained in that expression, "poetic traditions": the past, which to be perceived as such presupposes a break *and* continuity; and the association between poetry and something approaching the primitive. According to Herder, the national genius and the collective soul of every people are incarnated and expressed in the spontaneous manifestations of its art, which mark the beginnings of its history and survive wherever external and learned influences have been unable to penetrate.[12] Hence the combined interest in the poetry of the Middle Ages and in popular poetry, an interest that manifested itself in Germany with Herder himself, though his notion of *Volkslied* is oddly eclectic.[13] It is seen also and especially in Brentano, and to a lesser extent in Arnim, Uhland, the Brothers Grimm, of course, and even in Heine, who makes no scientific claims but who displays an acute irony and sensibility.[14] Mérimée perfectly and agreeably rendered that combination in depicting Professor Wittembach, the narrator of *Lokis*.[15] In France, Hersart de La Villemarqué[16] exhibited as if they were a miracle "popular Breton songs" that were an exact copy of Marie de France's lai *Laüstic* or of the encounter between Perceval and the knights in Chrétien de Troyes's *Conte du Graal* (The story of the Holy Grail).[17]

Do we have to pass through romanticism, then, and through German romanticism, to get to the literatures of medieval France? Yes, we do. It is these conceptions, inherited from Herder, that have given the studies of medieval philology and literature the responsibility for defining the identity of the peoples of Europe, in both senses of the word *identity*: what distinguishes them and what unites them.[18] For what distinguishes them is the lesser or greater capacity to keep not only their primitive genius but also the trace of an original, paradisiacal, and lost unity, that of humanity at its beginnings. It is that theory that laid the groundwork for the association, still profoundly anchored today, between the Middle Ages and folklore. It is responsible for sustaining the enthusiasm of both general readers and philologists for a poetry perceived as naive. In nineteenth-century France, it is these ideas that accompanied the combined interest in German romanticism and the new philological methods practiced in German universities. To parody Martianus Capella, medieval studies were the offspring of the marriage of romanticism and philology.[19] It is that combination that pushed the first French medievalists to turn their gaze toward Germany and to deplore the fact that the study of our ancient language and literature was more developed there than in France. On 20 March 1852, Paulin Paris, assistant curator of manuscripts at the Bibliothèque Nationale, drafted a note requesting that a chair of French language and literatures of the Middle Ages be created at the Collège de France. Here is his first argument:

> That language and that literature have . . . [as is now known throughout Europe] precedence and preeminence over all other neo-Latin literatures. The French chroniclers, poets, and prose writers inspired the greatest geniuses of Germany, Italy, Spain, and Belgium; and France alone seems to be refusing the homage everyone is paying to her genius in literary initiative, by excluding from higher education that great and curious source of studies.[20]

Paulin Paris adds that he would not be unworthy to occupy that chair himself were it to be created. As we know, he obtained satisfaction on both points. A few years later, he sent his son and future successor, Gaston Paris, to Bonn, where he studied with the Romanist Friedrich Diez.[21]

Some will object that, in spite of everything, that is granting too much to romanticism and Germany. During the Enlightenment, a form of Italian patriotism already animated the medieval research of Muratori.[22] And in France, from Fauchet to Du Cange the interest in medieval history and mores, but also in letters, never died out completely.[23] In the course of the eighteenth century, the Académie des Inscriptions et Belles Lettres encouraged works devoted to the Middle Ages; foremost among these were works by La Curne de Sainte-Palaye.[24] We know the vastness of the medieval collection in the *Bibliothèque universelle des romans* (Universal library of romances).[25] We know the importance that Montesquieu's *L'esprit des lois* (The spirit of laws) grants to Frankish and Carolingian legislation in the constitution of French law. We know that Chateaubriand's *Génie du christianisme* (Genius of Christianity), which viewed the Middle Ages as "the only poetic time of our history," proposes a medieval and Christian model. Its ideological coloration is already perceptible in one of Baculard d'Arnaud's short stories and in one of Mme de Genlis's novels,[26] which dress up the misfortunes of emigration in medieval finery.

Setting aside more illustrious works, we might note that in 1826 the academician Parseval—almost Perceval!—published *Philippe Auguste, poème héroïque en douze chants* (Philip Augustus, epic poem in twelve cantos). In the first canto, the advice of the gods is replaced by advice from the fairies—evil fairies in fact, anti-French and pro-English—presided over by Mélusine.[27] That lucky find sets the tone of the poem: it is an epic in the classical mode whose subject is medieval, the equivalent of Ronsard's *Franciade* or Voltaire's *Henriade*. Despite the author's scholarly scruples, the era represented hardly exerts more influence on the literary form than it does in Corneille's *Le Cid* or *Attila* or in Voltaire's *Zaïre*. Is that because the pitiful Parseval was a belated neoclassicist, a *chauve* from the battle of Victor Hugo's *Hernani*? Not at all. For does one find a reflection of medieval literary art in Hugo's own *Burgraves*? Does the poetry characteristic of each past age cast a different tint on the successive pieces in Alfred de Vigny's *Poèmes antiques et modernes* (Ancient and modern poems) or Hugo's *Légende des siècles* (The legend of the centuries)?[28] A little, but so very little. The Middle Ages might very well have furnished the themes of inspiration to French romanticism, but the idea, though widespread, that medieval literary monuments exude the pure, unrefined essence of poetry, that they can in that respect be compared to popular art, had little influence in actuality.[29] In addition, the idea was soon to be ridiculed. In the *Première Education sentimentale* (The first Sentimental education), the young Flaubert writes of one of his characters, a budding writer who had read Schelling and Herder but who has now returned to more healthy conceptions:

> He reread what he could understand of the bards and trouvères, and he frankly admitted to himself that one would have to be oddly constituted to find all that sublime, even as the real beauties he again saw in them struck him all the more.
>
> In sum, he made little of all the fragments of popular songs, translations of foreign poems, cannibal odes, Eskimo chansonettes, and the rest of the heretofore unseen hodgepodge with which we have been assaulted for the last twenty years.[30]

The increasingly thorough and precise knowledge of medieval literature, which the progress of philology allowed by the end of the century, led to such associations being challenged; but for the moment, that progress itself had little influence on aesthetic reflection. Gaston Paris maintained that the place of medieval literature in teaching "ought to remain carefully limited," since "it does not correspond to the requirements of classical taste."[31] Yet he was ever intent on marking the place of his discipline within the historical sciences and within the perspective of history, intent as well, in the spirit of his time, on seeing literary history take root as a science, at the expense of rhetoric. But he did not go so far as to include aesthetics in the field of his historical reflection. He was interested—too much, his successors would say—in the link between the literature of the Middle Ages and popular poetry, and he was very sensitive to the charm of the latter, which he saw as "the faithful and spontaneous expression of French genius."[32] But he hardly sought to ground that link and that admiration in theory. For him, as for the obscure Parseval sixty or eighty years earlier, the Middle Ages could be an object of study, even of inspiration, but its poetic forms were in no case a model. The historical remoteness of the literary past did little to nourish his reflection on the essence of poetry as such.

Gaston Paris was still marked by his romantic conceptions, which inspired his theories of the epic cantilena and of the Indian origin of the fabliaux. His immediate successors, heirs to positive criticism who were accustomed to grounding hypotheses only in precise texts, were faithful to him even in opposing him. Joseph Bédier defended theses opposed to his in every field, always placing the emphasis on the deliberate character of literary creation and the decisive role played by particular individuals, great personalities, genius, in the origination and evolution of poetic forms.[33] That attitude does not simply express the desire to take into account only extant documents and to reject unverifiable hypotheses grounded in a faith in the existence of a continuous oral tradition, inaccessible by definition. It also reflects Bédier's affirmation of a certain conception of poetry. That was the sort of man he was, gifted with an exceptional sensitivity to texts. His conception is also dated, however. It belongs to the first part of the twentieth century, which tended to glorify or sanctify the poet, even while attributing to poetry an extreme self-consciousness, marked by the labor it imposes. Such a conception also presupposes a permanence of aesthetic values, those of poetic genius and labor, and is not essentially concerned with integrating a reflection on time as a constitutive factor of those values.

Without being guided in the least by a taste for provocation or a love of paradox, we can measure the originality of the romantic position by comparison. We may have some idea of the productiveness that a reflection by medievalists on the third age of Hegelian aesthetics—the romantic age, the age of subjectivity, which appeared with Christianity and whose true birth occurred with the Middle Ages—might have had if it had materialized. This was hardly the case, however, despite the atypical example of Benedetto Croce. We catch ourselves regretting the fact that we are unable to embrace the romantic vision of the Middle Ages, though it is erroneous on almost every point. For the interest manifested by that form of thought in the medieval past is altogether historical, since what was at stake was the interpretation of the history of peoples. Yet the historical was grounded in poetics. In a sense, poetics illuminated history and not the reverse. The understanding of history occurred through philology, through the attention granted to the formation of the idiom and the birth of the literature, through a reflection, that is, on language and aesthetics. Still, it is quite true that such a reflection, grounded in the belief that one finds "the people" by moving back in time, seeks the essence of poetry in its original, primary, elementary impetus rising up from buried depths—with all the associations of simplicity and primitivity, antiquity and archaism, that Flaubert makes fun of.

Yes, there was truly something at stake in the study of medieval literatures at that time, namely, the understanding of the spirit of peoples and the nature of poetry. Within that perspective, the first manifestations of the literatures of Europe took on an extreme importance, a greater importance in a sense than their subsequent development, since they were supposed to reflect a state of art when genius had not yet been superseded—but also crushed—by taste.[34] But what of all that today? Who still believes that the national identity of peoples is revealed in their first artistic productions and that these productions are collective and spontaneous? No one. Who would call medieval literature popular? No one. The development of philology made quick work of dissipating the romantic illusions that had encouraged philology in the first place. And yet, even then, the stakes of these studies do not seem to have disappeared; the interest they awakened did not flag. Why? Why did the fascination exerted by this literary past outlive the philosophical foundations that had elicited and justified it? Was it because, during that period of Franco-German conflicts, national quarrels broke out on the debris of romantic thought, with each nation seeking superiority in the precedence or preeminence of its literature? These preoccupations existed, it is true, and sometimes among the greatest medievalists, but it would be wrong to exaggerate them. It might be more correct to invoke, here as in every discipline, the positivist faith in knowledge for itself and the conviction—perhaps unjustified—that everything that can be known deserves to be known.

But the question raised is not resolved for all that. Why has there been an effort to know, before anything else, what there was *before* what we already know or before what we think we already know? Why that interest, which was for decades almost exclusive, in the insoluble question of origins: the origins of the chansons de geste, of the lyric forms, of courtly love, the sources of the Breton romances? We might, of course, invoke the constant tendency to seek in every beginning—of the universe, of life, of civilization—a key to ourselves and in the past a justification for our own choices, as if that past resonated with our personal past and our own childhood. And it is true that the Middle Ages, which are so closely tied to childhood, were for two centuries conscripted under various ideological banners. But beyond that response, which is too general and too easy, an examination of the mechanisms by which medieval literature grounds its effects would no doubt make it clear that the prehistory of literature is above all a trompe l'oeil creation of literature itself. It is the texts themselves that send their reader on a wild goose chase for their antecedents.

This trompe l'oeil probably exists in every age and in every literary system. It corresponds to an aesthetic necessity and an expectation. But the Middle Ages, an age in effect marked by the signs of the beginning, by the anguish of rupture and the concern for continuity, play on that effect with predilection. The romantic, in quest of the roots of a collective identity; the philologist, in search of positive sources; the anthropologist, on the trail of primitive forms of art and of the imaginary—all found in medieval literature a field that was especially promising in that, for centuries, it had held out a mirror that sent back a reflection of their own illusions. True illusions, however, since these false perspectives are truly set up by that literature.

That is the first proposition I would like to advance today. The second is that this true illusion, this illusion through which the nature of the object that elicits it reveals itself, also presents itself to the ethnologist and the folklorist. Thus the tenacious association between the literature of the Middle Ages and folklore is something completely different from a deplorable relic of romantic thought. If every conjuration in the last century has been powerless to dissipate it, it is for excellent reasons; but it is not because folklore—whatever name we give it or whatever reality we designate by that name—might offer a kind of explanation for medieval literature. The third proposition is that it is in the nature of literature itself to produce such an illusion, and to such an extent that we may seek in that illusion a criterion for defining literature itself.

The literature of the Middle Ages constantly refers to its own past; that much is obvious. But that it weaves its own background canvas before taking its pose in front of it, that it gives the appearance of depth to a stage set it has itself painted—that would seem to be an arbitrary supposition. For after all, the vast Latin domain of that literature was in fact a continuation of ancient letters—pagan, biblical, patristic—and rightly presented itself as their descendant even as it assured their continued life. The same is true of large swaths of vernacular literature constructed on Latin models. Of course, between the end of the ninth century and the end of the eleventh, following the appearance of the Romance languages and their accession to the field of writing, new forms emerged and blossomed in the manner familiar to us. But it would be just as unreasonable to deny their roots in a tradition that, to a great degree, necessarily escapes us as it would be to reduce them to the emergence in writing of such a tradition. Let us consider matters from a different angle. Why are we endlessly driven to suppose that a tradition escapes us? Why, as we move from one text to another until we reach the most ancient one, do we always have the feeling that we stand on the threshold of the enigma? Because the texts proliferate with signs that make that feeling take root in us. And they do not simply emit those signs. They sow them and arrange them in such a way as to submit their effects to the requirements of a poetics that is of their time and not inherited from the past.

That is also true of many manifestations of Romance lyricism, whose origins are so intriguing and in which the contrast between learned courtly poetry and the simplicity of so-called women's songs has been so striking. Some have seen in these women's songs the vestiges of an ancient tradition, issuing from the depths of the people, which the new, demanding, and complex art of the troubadours covered over, before allowing them to surface again in bits and pieces. Perhaps that is true. What is certain, however, is that medieval literary art took great care to obtain effects of contrast by conferring on one part of the lyric production marks of simplicity and *rusticitas*, and that, in order to do so, it inserted signs that associate that production with the past. No matter how far back in time we go, we see at every moment of literature, in successive synchronic strata, the poetic system integrating songs into its overall operation, songs that are consistently marked by the same signs. These signs set them off from the rest of poetry, which is concerned with refinement and novelty. What are these signs? They are the signs of fragmentation and discontinuity, which produce two effects. First, the effect of quotation: The song exists only between learned brackets. And second, the effect of the trace: The fragment is unfailingly perceived as a vestige of a disappeared whole.

"No matter how far back in time we go": That formulation ought to be understood literally. Some of the most ancient extant texts in a Romance language appear as fragments of songs cited in entirely different poems, written in a different language. These are the *khardjas*, which conclude the Andalusian *muwwashahs*. Some of the *khardjas* are not in Arabic—or in Hebrew—like the rest of the poem, but in the Mozarabic dialect, the Romance language of the indigenous population, the Christians of Spain.[35] All these Mozarabic *khardjas* suggest in a few words the lament of a young woman in love: "O you who are dark, o delight to the eyes! Who can bear absence, my love?" Everything works to create a sharp contrast between the poem and that final touch: the change of language, of style, of subject matter. But it is the contrast that foregrounds the aptness of the quotation. The greater the distance between the poem and its *khardja*, the more ingenuity and wit the poet needed to dare the brevity of a juxtaposition that is at once pertinent and audacious. The *khardja* that concludes and simultaneously grounds—metrically and musically—a new, brilliant, complex poem must appear fragmentary, stuttering, issued from the fount of ages and the depth of the soul. It must appear to be of an insistent, overdetermined simplicity: the simplicity of a language that is not an educated language, of a rudimentary poetics, and of the ignorant young woman who makes her voice heard.

One cannot seek to reconstitute a past of which these Romance *khardjas* would be both the endpoint and the monuments: they emerge from a universe that escapes us. Some of them have obviously been remodeled, if not invented, by the Arab poet who cites them. But they find their place within a poetics that puts them to use by playing on fragmentary quotation and cultural distance, giving them the coloration of a traditional art in contrast to a learned art.

Far from being unique, this type of effect reappears constantly in the subsequent Middle Ages, and within the Romance world itself. At the beginning of the thirteenth century, it is no doubt that effect that made for the success, and the limited success, of *chansons de toile*,[36] with their little old tune, their strophe similar in its simplicity to the epic laisse, their elliptical and stiff narration, and the grave young woman they show more skillful at needlework than at the artifices of a lover's discourse, who knows no more than to offer herself in silence to a nonchalant seducer. All these characteristics oppose the *chanson de toile* to courtly lyricism, but certain details—a trait of mores, a suddenly flowery melody, a labored imitation of the epic style—lead us to suspect a forced archaism. The roguish Jean Renart takes great care to display both the antiquity and the old-fashioned character of the *chansons de toile*. When he inserts them into his *Roman de la rose ou de Guillaume de Dole*, he has them sung by an old woman living in the most remote provincial castle. She herself says: "Ladies and queens of days gone by were always singing spinning songs as they embroidered."[37] In counterpoint, at court the emperor's jongleur sang an exaggerated and vaguely bawdy pastiche of them.[38] It is plausible that these songs are in fact linked to an ancient tradition. But it is above all obvious that they claim for themselves the characteristics of antiquity, simplicity, and even awkwardness. In the first third of the thirteen century, a public accustomed to the sophistication of the *grand chant courtois* found them charming. It was the charm of archaism, on which they played, the charm of the fragmentary, which was associated with them and expressed itself in their mysterious laconism and their knowing tone (*ton entendu*)—*entendu*, which is to say, *déjà entendu*, already heard. And what is a song, if not a *ton entendu*?

In this set of lyric forms that constitute a balance of contrasts, we find the same aesthetic effects that existed three centuries earlier in the *muwwashah*. The only difference is that the opposition between cultures and languages, which had disappeared, has been replaced by an insistence on the remoteness of the past. The notions of simplicity, tradition, archaism, antiquity, and naivete are beginning to be associated with one another.

Let us go even further. Songs conserved in collections from the second half of the fifteenth century have often been designated popular.[39] The manuscripts are carefully prepared, even sumptuous. Formally, many of these songs are hardly different from those that sustained the polyphony of the Burgundian court during the same era. They are sometimes identical.[40] Thematically, they display continuity with the learned lyric genres of the trouvères. What, then, is popular about them? Only the fact that they continue this tradition of the trouvères, a learned tradition if ever there was one, but an already ancient tradition abandoned by the court poetry of their time, which was avid for rhetorical, metrical, linguistic, and musical novelty. In contrast to that poetry, these songs in the manner of yesteryear, these strophic, monodic songs filled with spring gardens, nightingales, and roses gathered by shepherdesses, combine simplicity and the evocation of the past. They are sometimes mutilated, sometimes incoherent. They appear to be vestiges, and they privilege a rustic universe. They perpetuate slight archaisms of language that will later appear characteristic of popular literature. They thus invite confusion between ancient tradition and popular roots. In giving the illusion of a refreshing plunge into a rural past, they compensate for and balance out the stilted aridity of the learned poetry of their time. We should therefore not be astonished to see them collected in beautiful manuscripts, since they are the necessary complement of court poetry and in that respect belong to it.

It would be easy to continue to the modern era. Is it necessary to invoke Marot, who links young love and old songs?

> La chanson est (sans en dire le son):
> "Alegez moy, doulce, plaisant brunette."
> Elle se chante à la vieille façon.
> Mais c'est tout ung, la brunette est jeunette.[41]

> The song is (without telling its sound):
> "Relieve me, sweet and pleasing brunette."
> It is sung in the old fashion.
> But it's all the same, the brunette is quite young.

Is it necessary to cite another "old song," that of Molière's Alceste, the simple song in which "passion speaks . . . so pure," the song that attests to an art that is crude, ancient, and at the same time superior to the learned and corrupt art of today, with its "figural style" and its "trinkets": "The rhyme is not rich and the style is old"; "Our fathers, so completely crass, had much better [taste]."[42] In his idealization, Alceste confuses antiquity and naive simplicity, as Rousseau would soon do in *La nouvelle Héloïse* (The new Heloise): "Most of these songs are old romances whose tunes are not captivating, but they have something ancient and sweet about them that is touching after a time. The words are simple and naive."[43]

Is it necessary to evoke Nerval, who makes the songs of the Valois, which he cites only in bits and pieces, serve as a counterpoint to travels in the land of his childhood, to his childhood memories, to his forays into history, in short, to the lacunary outcrop of a hazy past coming to consciousness?[44] Is it necessary to recall the delicious lines in which George Sand remembers the impression produced on the little girl she once was by the enigmatic and melancholic suspense in the song *Nous n'irons plus au bois, / Les lauriers sont coupés*?[45] The sign of the past is oblivion. The songs must be fragmentary so that people will suppose them half disappeared, on the point of being lost.

And even so, we have limited ourselves to the example of lyricism. There are many others. "The rhyme is not rich," said Alceste, who makes of poverty richness. Similarly, we find that chansons de geste cling to assonance, even though they seem to have fallen very quickly under the spell of rhyme. We find that, confronted with the new fashion for the alexandrine, to which they nonetheless cede at times, they preserve the epic decasyllable in spite of everything. We find they allow themselves to be contaminated by the fashion for romance narrative, but not without mounting a resistance. We see them pre-serve their initial identity longer than any other genre, as if they knew that their appeal lay in their roughness, as if they defined themselves with respect to other genres by their rustic conservatism. Gregory Nagy has lent solid support to a similar hypothesis regarding Greek epic poetry and its relation to lyricism.[46] In the concert of literary forms, the epic part would be that of simple harmonies and affected dissonances. The famous cantilena of Saint Faron—a fake historically speaking, which guarantees its poetic truth—cultivates these har-monies and dissonances within the Latin world itself, which was on the point of exploding even before Romance literature appeared. It shows a remarkably accurate feeling for what Paul Zumthor calls—how can we resign ourselves to say "called"?—"the swerve" (*l'écart*).[47]

But might that insistent and illusory trace of the past not be itself an illusion? How are we to be certain that the texts truly aim for the effects that are here attributed to them, if they never explicitly signal their intention to make use of them? As it happens, there is one text, also very well known—too well known—and endlessly glossed, which clearly designates the artifice the literary work uses to draw its justification from a past whose contours are drawn only in the writ-ing itself and whose writing simultaneously blurs the contours. That is the prologue to Marie de France's *Lais*.[48] The argument of this pro-logue is familiar: The ancients composed deliberately obscure works, counting on time and the increasing penetration of their readers to draw out the meaning. Marie first thought of devoting herself to a translation from Latin into French. In the place of such an ordinary project, she undertook to transcribe Breton lais she had heard, so that they would not sink into oblivion. It is clear that, in her mind, the translation from Latin she abandoned would have resulted from the slow and progressive elucidation of classical literature as she first defined it; she thus grants a hermeneutic value to *imitatio*. It is also clear that she judges her two projects—the one she abandoned and the one she completed—as comparable. The obvious conclusion is that a new work is the heir and endpoint of works from the past and that it sets itself the task either of opening up their meaning or of saving their memory. In the first case, the veil of the *integumentum* can be lifted only by the passing of time, which in the second case threatens the survival of the lais.

In reality, it is Marie's prologue itself that projects behind it the shadow of a doubt—doubt born of the uncertainty of meaning or of the fragility of memory—and that claims to draw its raison d'être and its appeal from that doubt. The text comes into being by positing both the existence of a model drawn from the past and its lacunae, in such a way that neither can be separated from what the text itself is. It would be pointless to go looking for the model without that text. One would find only the obscurity of meaning or of oblivion. In the same way, in *Le lai du Chèvrefeuille* (The lai of the honeysuckle) by the same author, it is impossible to distinguish the inscription-vestige engraved on the hazelnut stick surrounded by honeysuckle, or perhaps merely signified by it, from the commentary that claims to fit perfectly into it and to develop it but which in fact feeds on it and absorbs it to the point of preventing it from being identified.[49] Of course, to return to the prologue of the *Lais*, Latin literature exists. Breton lais probably as well. The new work is in fact grounded in these prior models. But it takes shape only by singeing the fabric of their forms and tossing them back into the shadow, while at the same time exhibiting them in that indistinct state.

It may do so by surveying the entire set of literary forms existing at a particular moment. It may do so by using the swerve of quotation or by playing on the model's remoteness. Medieval literature pencils shadows in everywhere, arranges perspectives that suggest the remoteness of the past. At every period of its history, a part of itself affects an archaic simplicity and thus stands in opposition to the novelty claimed by the other part. To do that, it takes on the appearance of fragmentation and discontinuity, symptoms of an oblivion that is itself the mark of the past; it plays with poetic and linguistic effects, supposed to place it *juxta rusticitatem*, as Hildegaire says of his cantilena of Saint Faron. From the *khardjas* of Andalusia to the songs of the Valois, we have continually observed that the suggestions of incompletion, of rustic simplicity, and of archaism are intertwined. Such effects lead us back to our second proposition, which is, you will recall, that the illusory depth of the past also presents itself to the ethnologist and the folklorist.

Our brief jaunt of a moment ago through the songs and the centuries already illustrated that proposition. Everything I have put forth to this point has amounted to applying to literature the famous formulation that traditional societies "invent traditions in order to justify innovation."[50] Of course, the temporal permanence of narrative or poetic themes, like their extension in space, is not an illusion but a fact. It is not this fact that is being examined here but the fascination it exerts. It is not only romanticism that illusorily seeks the truth of popular culture and the traces of its now vanished coherence in the past. Even contemporary ethnology, though little inclined to naivete, has difficulty giving up that search. Researchers in the field always have the impression that they have arrived just a little too late, that the object they are pursuing is already half vanished, but that some traces of it persist. And their informers share that impression, suggest it to them. Singers of both sexes, storytellers of both sexes have always protested that songs and tales have been lost, and recently lost, that the singers or storytellers themselves have retained only odds and ends of them, but that that universe was still alive during their own youth: "My dear mother, yes! She filled up a sack with the bottom cut out. But for me, it's gone: the stories—I let them trickle away." Such are the words attributed by Henri Pourrat to the typical storyteller.[51] Whether at the dawn of the nineteenth century or the end of the twentieth, the discourse is the same. It thus has more to do with representation than with reality. Representation of what? Of the past. There again, oblivion guarantees antiquity. To quote Nicole Belmont's formulation, "the ideology of the good old days," "the illusion that the productions[,] . . . in tatters in our own time, were in the past coherent," is always present.[52] Boas, in a passage cited and commented on by Lévi-Strauss, observes that myth always appears as a relic and a fragment.[53] The ethnological object assumes its form under the gaze of the person who studies it, only by inviting that gaze to direct itself toward the past. In our civilization, the ethnologist engaged in this game quickly finds common ground with the medievalist, who is exposed to the same vertigo by the texts before his eyes.

Thus we see the ethnologist led to wonder what his object was before the moment he seized it, and tempted to believe that, had he only arrived a bit sooner, everything would have been explained. In the same way, the medievalist is led to suppose that the most ancient text he has before him is only the sequel, the trace, the scattered members of a text, of an oral production, or even of a myth, that is still more ancient, lost, or disfigured. If only he knew the *Chanson de Roland* that preceded the *Chanson de Roland*, the legend of Tristram before Béroul and Thomas, the Celtic source of Geoffroy of Monmouth, the book on the Holy Grail that Philippe d'Alsace showed Chrétien de Troyes, the lost poems of Eble de Ventadour, the strophic models of William IX, the songs from which the *khardjas* were excerpted! So it is that the storyteller erects into an index of tradition the shipwreck of memory, just as Marie de France erected the oblivion that threatened Breton lais. So it is that myth claims to be dismembered by time, offering itself to the sagacity of its interpreter, just as classical literature, again according to Marie de France, has to cower in the shadow of the past so that a gloss can come to illuminate and complete it.

There is nothing astonishing, then, in the fact that the association between medieval literature and ethnological literature has outlived the hypothesis that both are collective and spontaneous productions that reveal a national identity. That is because the association was primary. Far from stemming from that hypothesis, the association, within particular historical and ideological circumstances, suggested it in the first place. At its root is the impression that both kinds of literature retain the more or less indistinct traces of a past and that a knowledge of that past would reveal their secret. That past grounds their authenticity. The impression is indestructible, for it is on the order of the poetic. Once more, it is an effect produced by the works themselves, an effect made perceptible by the contrast with other works, which produce a different effect. Which other works? The part of medieval literature that makes a claim for novelty and sophistication: the official, canonical, learned literature, "great literature"— or, more simply, the literature of the field researcher. Without that opposition, ethnological literature, or so-called popular literature, would not be perceived as literature. But if such is the case, that effect is one of the components making up the very definition of literature. That is our third proposition. If it is well founded, that notion of "literature," whose very application to the Middle Ages seemed problematic a little while ago, takes shape only by appealing to a particularly remarkable trait of medieval letters.

Let us summarize our observations one last time. The literary art of every era takes care to mark certain productions with signs that associate them with the past. These signs include explicit references to the past, of course, but they are not limited to them. They are also signs of simplicity and rusticity, in accordance with the implicit hypothesis of a progressive refinement of letters. Finally, they are signs of fragmentation, producing in this respect a dual effect, of quotation and of relic. They thus suggest that these productions are residues of a buried whole from the past, and they anticipate the association between the archaic and the popular. The productions marked, depending on the era, as archaic, popular, or both at the same time, and which pretend to be out of fashion and beyond time, are opposed to others, felt to be learned, new, and fashionable, which constitute the core of intellectual and literary life and confer its brilliance on it. The most apparent function of these first works is to provide contrast to the set of literary forms as a means of balancing them and bringing them into relief and to create a perspective of rootedness and evolution. The ideological representation that such a system does not fail to elicit would thus be subordinated to aesthetics and not the reverse.

But we might also recognize in these productions another function, which, in the equilibrium of the literary system, would place them not on the margins but in the center. They would not be merely the shadow charged with bringing out the light but in some way the very conscience of literature, the reminder of what it is in its essence. Is it so absurd, in effect, to apply to literary activity in itself the traits that define *la pensée sauvage*, thought in its wild state, according to Lévi-Strauss: namely, the activity of the sign rather than the concept, the grounding of its effects and its discourse to a great extent in analogy?[54] There is, then, nothing surprising in the fact that literature feels the need to recall that it is fundamentally in league with something primitive, just as poetry is perpetually led to situate itself in relation to intellectuality and to confront it. Perhaps literature, whose task is to give words their proper weight, sees itself and saw itself confusedly as a permanent struggle against the leveling of the signs of language, as nostalgia for an ancient state in which, as Lévi-Strauss would also say, they were not only signs but values as well, both richer and more awkward than what a more perfect adequation to the needs of communication has produced.[55] Literature would thus find at every moment the justification for its existence only to the extent that a part of itself would bring out, by effects of contrast, the trace of a past in which it claims to be grounded. Is it not true that the metaphor of the imaginative and irrational childhood of peoples, and the conviction of the imagination's roots in memory—to use Vico's manner of expression—find their best justification in literary productions, which continue to provide them with a general confirmation but also with a contradiction in the particulars? On one hand, literary productions endlessly refer to that childhood and credit the idea that "the world in its childhood was composed of poet peoples," as one of Vico's axioms, this time quoted verbatim, would have it.[56] On the other hand, when examined closely and taken in their singularity, such productions are all situated beyond such a childhood and designate it or appear to keep the trace of it only through conscious artifice.

To return to the sources of medieval studies and of the present essay: Must we therefore invoke the famous formulation of Hegel, that "art, from the point of view of its supreme destiny, is something of the past"? Within the framework of Hegelian aesthetics, outside of which it has no meaning, this formulation means that, since the advent of Christianity, art no longer has a vocation to reveal the truth of the world. In principle, then, Hegel's statement has nothing to do with the considerations we are discussing here. And yet, in the Hegelian division of history, not only does this statement apply to the modern period of art, of which the Middle Ages are the first original stage, it also supposes that a sort of nostalgia, and an anxiety about its ends, are inherent in art. It thus designates and associates two essential traits of medieval literature, the insistent allusion to its own past in tatters and the constant inquiry into its legitimacy with respect to faith. If art belongs to the past, it is because it has in some way been discredited by the present time of Revelation.

We can therefore add a new order of relations and contrasts to the order suggested here. It is not only a part of poetry that affects a turn toward the past so as to foreground another part, which makes a claim for novelty. Poetry as a whole, inasmuch as it makes claims to truth, finds itself cast into the shadows of the past by the light of Christian truth and derives its obscure attraction from being so relegated. The literary effect that opposes a suggestion of the residual and of the primitive to the claim for novelty draws its force from the implication that a truth lies buried in the past. Medievalists have responded by rushing to examine the prehistory of their texts. But the medieval reader could only measure that supposed truth against the only Truth. From the reflection on the proper and disconcerting character of pagan morality that marks certain adaptations of works from Antiquity, to the ambiguous effort to constitute a parallel history around the Holy Grail, that is, an archeology justifying Christian chivalry; from the fragment of a lover's cry, innocent and provocative—the troubadour's song—to the patient weaving of lyric wreaths for the Virgin: Everywhere we can detect the avowed, veiled, sometimes denied, often anguished concern to bring face to face "the love of letters and the desire for God," in the admirable and famous formulation of Don Jean Leclercq.[57] That love is nostalgia and that desire a hope, the intuition of a reminiscence that reveals each individual to himself, and the appeal to a truth that wrests him away from himself. The expression of faith endlessly affirmed in medieval letters is thus not the insipid gangue that surrounds and dissimulates the nuggets of pure poetry, not signs revealing profound mind-sets and buried myths. That is not only because such an expression of faith is the only thing that allows us to take the proper measure of the relation between the Latin world and the vernacular domain, but also because it points out and mirrors the contrast that shapes the reliefs of literature by inscribing within it the vanishing lines of a trompe l'oeil past.

Trompe l'oeil, illusion: One might object that the share granted to impression is too great. Have I nothing more solid to present? No, because nothing is more solid than impression. Of course, the positive knowledge of medieval literature progresses, and that is fortunate. Dates, attributions, locations become more precise and more certain. The history of texts is clarified. Discoveries occur: have not 154 lines of Thomas's *Tristan* recently been found?[58] But the share of conjecture remains great, and many uncertainties are definitive. In contrast, impression indubitably exists. Obviously, it deceives us. The Middle Ages are a distant age and they have become foreign to us. If they appear close to us, that is illusion—an indubitable truism that is gravely repeated to us. But that illusion is true, since we are its victims. It deserves to be confronted with the facts as we know them, as we reconstitute them, as we suppose them to be. Of course, the forms of thought and of sensibility have changed, as has their expression and the language itself. But must we therefore refuse to recognize that the Middle Ages remain half familiar to us? In addition, if it is true that the *right distance* is found only at the cost of successive, contradictory adjustments that are always being called into question, the person who bends down to look at the poetry of the past has no choice—unlike the historian perhaps—but to first run the risk of proximity. Of course, she does not claim to read the old texts as their contemporaries did or as their authors foresaw. It is only all the more miraculous that they still touch her. They do so at the price of misinterpretation: they lead her into error, but it is nonetheless true that they lead her there. Let us begin from that error, let us seek, in the Middle Ages and in ourselves, the truth of that error.

It is always a fragmentary truth—this fragmentation that is at the heart of literary art—but a truth whose search, for that very reason, procures a pleasure similar to that of art itself. It is a truth whose scattered pieces we interminably assemble but of which others besides us may have the dazzling revelation. A discouraging revelation for anyone who devotes his or her life to attempting, patiently and weightily, to reconstitute the aims, sense, and flavor of those distant texts. But a blessed revelation since, at the end of the labor, we have no other resource but to place our reliance in it. In the end, a voice other than that of the pedant must make these texts resonate, so that they may elicit the rapture and the meditation without which there can be no good reason to read them. In the end, we must listen to the voice of the poet:

> Iseult séjourne dans la salle basse très peu claire,
> Sa robe a la couleur de l'attente des morts,
> Et c'est le bleu le plus éteint qui soit au monde,
> Ecaillé, découvrant l'ocre de pierres nues.[59]

> Isolde dwells in the low and barely lighted room,
> Her robe the color of the dead awaiting
> And the faintest blue in the world,
> Flaking, uncovering the ocher of naked stones.

The medieval legend offers itself as a fresco half effaced by time. The "faint blue" color, the color of time itself, is flaking away. There are only traces of it remaining on the ocher of oblivion. The weak light, the drab and almost vanished color, "the dead awaiting," such is the mortal oppression that weighs upon Isolde's fate. Such is the threatened memory that medieval poems claim to preserve. Such is the threatened memory we keep of these poems and which bestows on them their value for us. Such is our image of the Middle Ages—dented capitals, bits of fresco emerging from under the whitewash—these Middle Ages that touch us only inasmuch as we perceive them as distant and hazy. It is Isolde, but in a later version it is "the orante." It is the past of legend and the expectation of prayer. It is a poem by Yves Bonnefoy. Our only fear is that the slavish gloss of medieval letters will never succeed in illuminating them in just that way.

Are the Songs of the Middle Ages Old Songs?

▮ *Preliminaries*

The title of this course—of this embryo of a course—falls short in several respects. First, we were once taught never to give a title the form of a question, if only because typography makes it impossible to punctuate. Second, that question appears stupid. The Middles Ages are nothing new, and its songs are indisputably old, at least in relation to a human life, human memory, and changing civilizations. But those of you who did me the honor of attending my inaugural lecture will detect what lies behind that bad question. Why the taste for old songs? Why seek in the Middle Ages the roots of French songs? Why link popular songs to those of the Middle Ages? But above all: Why in the Middle Ages themselves are certain songs adorned with the signs of antiquity, others with signs of novelty? Why, in the modern era, do certain songs refer back to the Middle Ages? And what are the signs of antiquity in particular, since only the present exists and the impression produced by a song, as by anything else, occurs in the present? Moreover—and here is another weakness of my title, or perhaps of the presentation itself—we will not speak of songs immediately but will get to them only after a few prolegomena. And even when we at last reach the songs, we will not speak immediately of the Middle Ages but will first take a detour through the modern era.

Finally, the title of the course could be criticized for a certain fuzziness, which this detour runs the risk of maintaining rather than dissipating. What are the medieval songs I propose to speak about? Until about 1150, all literature in the vernacular was sung. That is, in fact, one of the traits that might make the term *literature* inadequate when applied to the Middle Ages. Even much later in the medieval period, chanting, cantillation, psalmody, the resources of the voice in general, informed the greater part of literary expression.[1] And then, in the Middle Ages there were songs of every kind, from the chansons de geste to the troubadour cansos and including all the lyric genres. To begin with the modern era means maintaining the fuzziness, because it means beginning with a continuity or supposed association between popular songs and medieval songs, which was established by the romantics. That continuity or association itself implies a fuzzy vision of medieval literature and its songs. In returning to the Middle Ages, we will have the opportunity, I hope, to clarify our point of view. Of course, we will not be able to speak of everything, and we will, in fact, speak of very little. What we will say will hinge on lyric poetry. But from our perspective, to separate epic or narrative song from the outset from what is called by pleonasm lyric song would entail more disadvantages than an initial ambiguity.

According to Nietzsche, man is sick from his memory. He is unable to forget.[2] Literature is a symptom of that sickness. As a representation, it refers to what it represents and which by definition existed before it, hence to the past—in opposition, Hegel would say, to philosophy, which "has to do [only] with the *eternally present.*"[3] This sickness we cherish. Perhaps Ovid and his medieval imitators were wrong to say that love is the only illness of which one does not wish to be cured—a symptom that allows for an infallible diagnosis. For we no more want to be cured of memory and of literature than of love.[4]

That is our own illness. It is the illness that pushes me to speak of the poetry of the Middle Ages and which incites you to come and listen to me. I evoked that illness in my inaugural lecture by underscoring that, in a general way, literature in itself has something to do with the past. In the case of ancient and—precisely—medieval forms of this malady, I suggested that the literature of the Middle Ages it-self creates the signs that invite its reader to see it as a relic of the past, even as it lays the foundations for a new system. As I said at the time, on a different order this is somewhat like traditional societies, which "invent traditions in order to justify innovation." Medieval literature creates effects of trompe l'oeil perspective—which is a pleonasm, since every effect of perspective is a trompe l'oeil.

But that very metaphor, which imposes itself so spontaneously, re-veals a difficulty. For in the Middle Ages—who does not know this?—perspective in painting was poorly mastered or not at all mas-tered. Do we therefore need to change the metaphor? If the people in the Middle Ages knew nothing of perspective, then the image of a *vanishing line* did not impose itself upon them to define the vision or the representation of the past. For them, there were no successive planes moving back toward the depth of an uncertain distance. There was no blurring and shrinking of objects in the distance which, trans-posed from space to time, would suggest the inaccessibility of earlier eras. Since they did not have the capacity to represent perspective, how could they imagine a past that was neither effaced nor clear but shaded or dim, a past incorporated into the present like a distant background? How, in the succession of causes and their effects, could they even conceive that distance in time leads to a confusion of causes? If we must speak of trompe l'oeil, the type used in the Mid-dle Ages did not feign the false distance of perspective but the false chain of causality. As you may have gathered, what I am suggesting is no more than an extrapolation of Panofsky's famous demonstration. Not so much his reflection in *Perspective as Symbolic Form* as the strict demonstration of *Gothic Architecture and Scholasticism.*[5] As viewers follow with their eyes the groupings of branches and ribs back to the columns that support the edifice, they have the impression that they understand the structure and can visualize the way the mass is di-vided up. It is an illusion, for engaged colonettes, veins, intersecting ribs, far from being weight bearing, are only ornamental. Similarly, the dialectical divisions and articulations of scholastic argument give the impression that they are productive, that they engender the progression of thought. That is not at all the case, however; they are only an artifice of exposition.

The trompe l'oeil of Gothic architecture, like the illusions of scholastic thought, are on the logical order. Both consist of an appearance of logic that does not correspond to a true necessity. That false logic supposes an overvaluation of logic. On the other hand, perspective submits the rigor of logic to the rigor of error, to the rigorous harmony of perception—which would in a sense make scholastics Platonic and perspective Aristotelian. In a word, if medieval thinkers had had a knowledge of perspective, that is, of the distortion of vision in space, it would have suggested to them a distortion of vision in time, a manner of taking into account the vanishing lines of the past. Instead, they privileged the display of causality, which kept them from depicting causes distant in space or time as blurred. For them, the background was clear, for there was no background. They moved from one cause to the next, each cause ideally just as present to the gaze that isolated it as the preceding or following cause. Medieval schools, moreover, taught logic but not history.[6]

Medieval painters knew nothing of effects of perspective in the spatial order (since Saint Augustine, however, medieval writers had reflected on the fact that in the reality of vision distance dims outlines); nonetheless, these effects in the temporal order were known in their literary art. Not so much at its center, perhaps, in its vast and brilliant constructions, but at its margins, in fleeting and minor works. This literary art knew how to create vestiges by playing on shading and gradation—we cannot get away from pictorial metaphors, and every effort will be made to designate in their literal precision effects that are generally taken into account only figurally. These effects are more characteristic of songs than of stories, mythical accounts, or forms of narration or recitation which could be linked to story or myth through their avatars in romances, exempla, or hagiography. All these forms of narrative are, of course, rooted in the past—their action is generally situated in the past—but they somehow present themselves as perpetual re-creations. On one hand, the narrative may claim to be a new version of an old story, as is the case for the romances (and strictly speaking, the rewritings, compilations, and prose renderings from the end of the Middle Ages are nothing less). Whether it is ranging over as many generations as it likes, moving backward to the fathers' generation or ahead to the sons' (beginning with the generation of Arthur or Charlemagne), whether it is part of a chronology going from the Trojan War to William the Conqueror or from Joseph of Arimathea to Galahad, there is one thing that the romance does not take into account, and that is the possibility of forgetting. Merlin is always there to know everything and Blaise to write it down. Only the chansons de geste sometimes have a doubt, but then, they are *chansons*, songs. On the other hand, as often occurs in the exempla or the fabliaux, the narrative may claim to relate a recent, unique, real event, and it is we who detect a mythical substratum in it or who link it, spatially or temporally, to other similar or comparable narratives. But the form always claims to be new or renewed—adapted from Latin into Romance language in the first romances, from verse to prose in their later reworking, underscoring in relentlessly repeated formulae the need to follow the evolution of the French language, which, as Jean Molinet writes in 1500 in his prose rendering of the *Roman de la rose*, had become "very charming and new again."

The songs are another matter, however. And yet, do they not often, and in certain contexts almost systematically, claim to be new? Of course: It must therefore follow that there are old songs. In fact, there is a great deal to be said about that novelty itself, and we will try to say a bit about it later on. But other songs claim to be old: They play on memory and forgetting, play on the permanence that their form and melody suppose, play on the fact that their interpreter cannot claim to do anything more than actualize something preexistent. For Jean Renart, the first to insert songs into a romance and proud of it, that procedure entailed playing on the new and the old. Even the chansons de geste distinguish themselves from the rest of narrative literature by their ostentatious conservatism, by the fact that the one who utters them most often presents himself as only their interpreter and glories more in having properly retained an old song than in having properly told an old story. In a single gesture, these chansons de geste make a claim for a certain historicity and take on the trappings of vestiges. Some have wondered whether the chansons de geste might not go back to the Carolingian age, that is, to the time of the subject matter they treat. That question has never been raised in the same terms for romances, with respect to their Arthurian or ancient subject matter.

In examining the origins of lyricism, medievalists have, as if instinctively, always considered the medieval songs that most resembled "popular" songs (that is, songs dating from after the Middle Ages) older than the songs of the troubadours, or at least grounded in a more ancient tradition. This is because of the link made by the romantics between the popular and the past. Yet the troubadours' songs are more bewildering for the modern reader. They totally vanished from the literary landscape centuries ago. They nonetheless appear to be typical of the "new" song. In contrast, the songs that can be traced continuously to the modern age (from the death of the lovely Aude to *Belle Doette* and from *Belle Doette* to *Malborough s'en va-t-en guerre*, from the pastourelles to *Derrière chez nous y a un étang*), songs from the end of the fourteenth or fifteenth century, which have more or less survived until our time (*J'ai descendu dans mon jardin*, *La Péronelle*, *L'amour de moi si est enclose*, *Gentils gallans de France*), have for us the scent of antiquity. When, sniffing out that scent, medievalists have followed their tracks back to the thirteenth or even the twelfth century, they have then sought to go back even further, not realizing that this scent of the ancient is perceptible only in the present, since it is attached to the songs that have survived, not to those that have disappeared.

That is why, instead of taking things in chronological order, we will move backward in time. We will begin with the notion of popular song in the nineteenth and twentieth centuries, with the association between that notion and the Middle Ages, and will move back to the Middle Ages, following the aesthetic and poetic constants that are at the foundation of that notion and that association. That reverse chronology, however, will not be respected in the details. We will begin the modern age with the romantic notion of *Volkslied* and move forward over the last two centuries. Moreover, falling victim to the prestige of origins even as we claim to be liberating ourselves from it, we will first examine evidence from before romanticism.

Our plan will proceed as follows. We will first examine a few very well known *testimonia* dealing with popular songs, or what it is conventional to call such, *testimonia* dating from between the sixteenth and the nineteenth century. We will see how the notion of popular song has been increasingly associated with the impression of antiquity and with a feeling for the past. We will then look at how the discovery that the literature of the Middle Ages was not a popular literature led to a fracturing, then to a recomposition of these associations. Finally, after so many preliminaries—which are much more than preliminaries in every respect, however—we will return to the Middle Ages to show how medieval poetry in itself justifies that association.

I

"The Fairy of Legend, Eternally Young"

Popular Songs, Old Songs

Gascons and Cannibals

The examples to be examined are precisely those I briefly mentioned in my inaugural lecture. There is one example, however, which I did not speak of at that time, even though it is very famous and has been for a very long time. That, I confess, is because it does not support my argument, or rather because in order to integrate it into my demonstration I needed to supply a commentary that I could not give on that day but which will now be our concern.

At issue is a passage from Montaigne's *Essays*, book 1, chapter 54, "Of Vain Subtleties":

> Popular and purely natural poetry has spontaneous effects [*naïvetés*] and charms [*grâces*] by which it may be compared to the principal beauty of poetry as perfected according to art; as is seen in the villanelles of Gascony and the songs that are brought back to us from nations that have no knowledge of any science, or even of writing. Mediocre poetry, which stops between the two, is disdained and without value.[1]

This passage is the first in which the expression "popular poetry" appears in French (I say "in French," so as not to take into consideration expressions such as *carmen rusticum* and others). We therefore find it cited by all those concerned with popular songs: It was already cited by Hersart de La Villemarqué in the 1867 introduction to *Barzaz-Breiz*; it has been cited in our own time by J.-A. Bizet, by Miodrag Ibrovac, and by Paul Bénichou.[2] But above all, it was partially cited by Herder: It is the first of the testimonies on popular song (*Zeugnisse über Volkslieder*) placed at the beginning of his *Volks-lieder, Erster Teil* (Popular songs, part 1), published in 1778. His German translation of Montaigne, very accurate by the way, simply highlights the notion of nature more than the original, but consistent with it and in a significant way.[3] That is because, for Herder, nature and the forces of nature are the source of genius, to the point that genius becomes confused with them. To define, as he does, "the poetry of the people" (*Volkspoesie*) as "entirely nature" (*ganz Natur*) is to say that such poetry is the product of genius: "Genius is a union of natural forces: it thus comes from the hands of nature and must precede the appearance of taste."[4]

To return to Montaigne: Why did I at first miss the chance to cite a passage so well known and so remarkable, a passage judged fundamental by the very founder of the vogue for the *Volkslied*? Because its perspective is not at all chronological or evolutionist. It does not associate popular poetry with the poetry of the past. It does not seem to imply any evolution or any perfecting of poetry over time. Might I have thus committed the error of setting aside important evidence because it did not support my theory?

Before condemning me, look more closely at what Montaigne says. What defines popular poetry in his view is spontaneity. It is a "purely natural" poetry. In that respect, it stands opposed to poetry that knows and observes the rules of art ("perfected according to art"). Its qualities are *naïvetés* and *grâces*—the first of these terms is redundant with "purely natural," the second as well perhaps, if *grâces* have something to do with grace, which is maintained effortlessly. We understand why such a judgment held Herder's attention. But we may also be permitted to direct our attention elsewhere, reading further along in the passage and citing it more extensively than Herder did. We then see that *popular poetry* and *poetry as perfected according to art* are opposed, of course, but only to "be compared," that is, to find themselves on equal footing and to join together in their shared opposition to "mediocre poetry, which stops between the two." Popular poetry on one hand, poetry as perfected according to art on the other, have in common naivetes and graces that intermediate, mediocre poetry does not achieve. Why not? Clearly, even though the judgment is only implicit in this passage, because it strays off into *vain subtleties.* Hence we understand why that development, Montaigne's last addition to the text of the 1588 edition, was inserted into an essay that bears that title and whose first sentence, precisely, takes as an example of *frivolous and vain subtleties* a certain poetic virtuosity (calligrams or lines that all begin with the same letter). Montaigne finds some examples of that virtuosity among the Greeks, but it was also practiced in the Middle Ages, from beginning to end, from Carolingian poetry to the poems of the *grands rhétoriqueurs* (note that Paul Zumthor was interested in both):[5]

> There are some subtleties that are frivolous and vain, by means of which men sometimes seek commendation, like the poets who compose entire works in which every verse begins with the same letter. We see eggs, balls, wings, hatchets shaped by the Greeks of old with the measure of their verses, by lengthening some lines and shortening others so as to represent one or another of these figures.[6]

Popular and natural poetry, like poetry as perfected according to art, escapes such puerility. The two extremes meet. That is, in fact, the true lesson of this chapter, toward which it very quickly drifts and which all the examples illustrate:

> Women of quality are called *dames*; those of the middle class, *damoiselles*; and *dames* again, those of the lowest station. The canopies that are spread over tables are allowed only in the princes' houses and in taverns. Democritus used to say that gods and animals had more acute senses than men, who are on a middle level. The Romans wore the same attire on days of mourning and on

feast days. It is certain that extreme fear and extreme ardor of courage equally trouble and relax the bowels.[7]

The example of the two extremes of poetry thus corresponds to both themes of the chapter, that of vain subtleties and that of the meeting of extremes.

And what about time in all that? Of course, for an obvious reason to which we will return in a moment, Montaigne does not imagine a development of poetry over time. Conversely, he takes into account the time necessary for the formation of every mind and every poet in the shift from natural poetry to poetry as perfected according to art. The very expression "poetry as perfected according to art" presupposes a length of time devoted to an apprenticeship in the poetic arts, until they can be practiced to perfection. But this time of personal development, which separates the state of nature from the state of the educated man, is designated more explicitly in the lines that precede the passage cited by Herder. In the 1588 text, Montaigne develops the argument that will be taken up again by Pascal in the form: "A little knowledge turns one away from God, a great deal of knowledge brings one close to God." Simple minds and great minds, Montaigne says, share the same faith and are "good Christians," whereas "in the middle range of mental vigor and ability error of opinion is engendered." Thereupon, he introduces the last addition, including the considerations on poetry. It begins as follows:

> The simple peasants are good men, and good men the philosophers, at least what passes for philosophers in our time: strong and clear natures, enriched by a broad education in useful knowledge. The halfbreeds who have disdained the first seat, ignorance of letters, and have not been able to reach the other—their rear end between two saddles, like me and so many others—are dangerous, inept, importunate: these men trouble the world. Therefore for my part I draw back as much as I can into the first and natural stage, which for naught I attempted to leave.[8]

The passage on poetry with which we began immediately follows. From religion to instruction, and from there to poetry: Everywhere the same perfection—shared by the ignorant and the truly learned—stands opposed to the imperfection of the semilearned. Montaigne feigns to place himself in that last category. He claims he makes every effort to return to the natural state, for want of being able to accede to that of the truly learned man and the true sage. It is a contradictory effort, of course: How could one attain or rediscover a natural state by effort, hence artificially? All one can hope is that, at the price of that effort, one might reach a state that imitates that of nature, to the point of being mistaken for it. What is such a state, if not the height of art, the perfection of art? This illuminates in a peculiar way the considerations on poetry which immediately follow. For all of a sudden, it is not "popular and purely natural poetry" that achieves the quality of "poetry as perfected according to art" so much as the latter, whose perfection consists in recovering that of "popular and purely natural poetry," which would then be the true criterion for poetic perfection. For those who have left the state of nature, the goal would be to succeed in reconstituting nature to perfection and in producing a perfect simulacrum of it, after a long period of patience and through the effects of art.

To grasp Montaigne's idea, we need to say a word about the two examples of "popular and natural poetry" he provides. On one hand, there are the peasant songs of his region, the "villanelles of Gascony." A *villanelle* is a song of the *vilain*, the peasant. In that sense, the term is not medieval (in the Middle Ages, *vilanel* appears only as a derivation and synonym of *vilain*); it originated in the sixteenth century. It is probably linked to the Iberian *villancico* and, like it, would designate a genre of poem with refrain, similar to the rondeau or the virelay. What also leads me to assume this is the definition of Cotgrave, cited by Godefroy: "Villanelle, a countreydance, round, a song."[9] The naive graces that Montaigne finds in the villanelles thus rest on a certain rustic or village character but also, quite certainly, on those effects characteristic of songs, such as refrains, which are themselves perceived as rustic.

But the other example is much more interesting, and it foregrounds another aspect of the villanelles of Gascony. This is the ex-

ample of "songs that are brought back to us from nations that have
no knowledge of any science, or even of writing." By that, Montaigne
means the songs of "cannibals," that is, of American Indians, specimens of which he had heard from the mouth of the man who had
been brought to the French court. He had these specimens translated
and cited them with admiration in the chapter entitled "Of Cannibals" (bk. 1, chap. 31):

> I must cite some examples of [the cannibals'] capacity. Besides the
> warlike song I have just quoted, I have another, a love song, which
> begins in this vein: "Adder, stay; stay, adder, that from the pattern
> of your coloring my sister may draw the fashion and the work-
> manship of a rich girdle that I may give to my love; so may your
> beauty and your pattern be forever preferred to all other serpents."
> This first couplet is the refrain of the song. Now I am familiar
> enough with poetry to be a judge of this: not only is there nothing
> barbarous in this fancy, but it is entirely Anacreontic.[10]

That "cannibal ode," as Flaubert would later say, was in Montaigne's eyes not at all barbarous and was altogether Anacreontic. It is
thus evoked once more in the passage we are considering, as an example of the naive graces of popular and natural poetry. We now see
why his position could not be explicitly "evolutionist"—if such a
word is not absurd under the circumstances. In his view, the perfection of art and civilization lies in the past, in Antiquity, the touch-
stone of poetic taste, as we see in his reference to Anacreontic poetry.
Spontaneous poetry ignorant of the rules of art, but nonetheless bearing comparison to classical poetry, is, in contrast, a poetry of the present, that of the peasants of Gascony or the savages of the New World.
The poetic gifts of American Indians, like their humanity, their sense
of justice, and their intelligence, are measured by objective, universal,
and constant criteria.

There is nonetheless an underlying evolutionist perspective, and
there cannot fail to be. First, as we saw a moment ago, the move from
the state of the ignorant man to that of the learned man presupposes
the time of an individual evolution; and second, in the chapter "Of

Cannibals," there is a comparison between the state of the cannibals and that which reigned in the Garden of Eden or in the Golden Age. Cannibals are defined as a people without writing, an invention that appeared in the Old World at a given moment of the past and of history. In both cases, cannibal civilization is implicitly defined with respect to an evolution (but not a progress) of humanity. In a word, whether at the level of an individual life or of history, it takes time to attain the perfection of art, but that perfection is not really progress, since it consists solely in recovering, after the regression of the intermediate state, the natural perfection of a spontaneous poetry. It is time that adds art to nature. But nature always prevails over art: "It is not reasonable that art should win the point of honor over our great and powerful mother Nature."[11]

Contrary to appearances, the passage from Montaigne thus implies that "popular and natural poetry" is in league with the past. Even for him, songs suggest an association between the past, the people, and the spontaneous simplicity of the state of nature.

From Marot to Nerval

In my inaugural lecture, I mentioned a few examples of that association from between the sixteenth and the nineteenth century. Some, the best known, have been pointed out and commented on by many others besides me. They speak for themselves or require only the few words of commentary I provided at that time: for example, Alceste's song in *Le misanthrope* (The misanthrope)[12] or the passage from Saint-Preux's famous letter on the grape harvest in Rousseau's *La nouvelle Héloïse*. Allow me nevertheless to return briefly to others, and first to the charming epigram by Marot, composed, like so many others, for Anne d'Alençon:

> Huictain
> J'ay une lettre entre toutes eslite.
> J'ayme un païs et ayme une chanson:
> N est la lettre en mon cueur bien escripte,
> Et le païs et celuy d'Alençon.

La chanson est (sans en dire le son):
Allegez moy, doulce plaisant brunette.
Elle se chante à la vieille façon:
Mais c'est tout ung, la brunette est jeunette.[13]

Octet
I have a letter among all others elect.
I love a country and I love a song:
N is the letter in my heart inscribed,[14]
And the country is that of Alençon.
The song is (without telling its sound):
"Relieve me, sweet and pleasing brunette."
It is sung in the old fashion.
But it's all the same, the brunette is quite young.

As he admits in his epigram, Marot loved the song *Allegez moy, doulce plaisant brunette* (Relieve me, sweet and pleasant brunette) and within that song the initial line itself. Ten years before citing it in the octet, he had already inserted it into one of his own songs:

D'un nouveau dard je suis frappé
Par Cupido cruel de soy:
De lui pensois estre eschappé,
Mais cuydant fuyr me deçoy:
Et remede je n'apperçoy
A ma douleur secrette,
Fors de crier: Allegez moy,
Doulce plaisant Brunette!

Si au Monde ne fussiez point,
Belle, jamais je n'aymerois:
Vous seule avez gaigné le poinct,
Que si bien garder j'esperois:
Mais quant à mon gré vous aurois
En ma chambre seullette,
Pour me venger, je vous feroys
La couleur vermeillette.[15]

With a new arrow I am struck
By Cupid cruel for his own sake:
From him I thought I had escaped

But in believing I was fleeing I deceived myself:
And remedy I see none
To my secret sorrow
Except to cry: Relieve me,
Sweet and pleasing brunette!

If in the world you were not,
My beauty, never would I love:
You alone have won the point,
I hoped so well to guard against:
But if as I desire I should have you
In my lonely chamber,
To seek revenge, I would make you
Turn the color of crimson.

As for the song *Allegez moy, doulce plaisant brunette* itself, we know it through a collection that was printed much later; it dates from 1638. Proof that these songs could have a long life before being written down. Were it not for Marot, we would not know that this one, far from being composed in the seventeenth century, was already an old song, or at least could present itself as such, in the 1530s. Here is the song:

Allegez moy douce plaisant brunette,
Allegez moy de toutes mes douleurs.
Vostre beauté me tient en amourette,
Allegez moy.
Si vous tenoy un mois ou quinze jours,
Je vous feroy, je vous feroy,
Non feroy, si le feroy,
La couleur vermillette,
Allegez moy.[16]

Relieve me, sweet and pleasing brunette,
Relieve me of all my suffering,
Your beauty holds me in fleeting love
Relieve me.
If I held you a month or a fortnight
I would make you, I would make you,
I would not make you, yes I would make you
Turn the color of crimson,
Relieve me.

The song is a rondeau: an initial refrain, a brief stanza interrupted by the insertion of the beginning of the refrain, which is repeated in its entirety at the end. And the rondeau is a song: In addition to the refrain, the stanza contains, in the style of a song, a sort of secondary interruption, a repetition and a hesitation. Under the circumstances, its false timidity increases the effect of roguish insinuation: "Je vous feroy, je vous feroy, / Non feroy, si le feroy."

Marot cited this song twice within an interval of ten years. It was running through his head. But from one instance to the next, he did not make the same poetic use of it. It is as if, with time, he had deciphered the nature of the pleasure it procured for him. The first time Marot used it, he made it a kind of paraphrase within a poem that was itself defined as a song and whose last lines were based on those of its model, though they were not an exact reproduction. As for the refrain, it became his own cry, a quotation of his own words and, at the same time, of the song from which he was borrowing them. In addition, he placed that refrain at the end of the stanza. Thus he kept its status as a refrain in two ways. For in the medieval tradition, there are songs in which each stanza ends with a different refrain. These refrains, rather than being defined by repetition, are so designated in that they present themselves as quotations, placed in the mouth of the poet or of a character. Thus, as poetry had often done before him, Marot uses effects of quotation, of reminiscence, and of poetic dialogue; but he does not comment on them, does not take any distance from them, does not accentuate them by showing he is aware that he is resorting to them. In fact, he does not even signal that he is using them. In short, he proceeds with a kind of timidity. He does not cast an external, superior, emotional, or condescending gaze on the poem. He turns it to his own account; he seems to place himself inside the form of art of which it is a specimen. He seems simply to move in what he believes is an upward direction by giving his own song a more mannered turn, one more consistent with the rules of great poetry. He shows respect for the hierarchies and conventions of poetic language, which is another sort of timidity.

But in the epigram, his attitude has changed a great deal. The song, like the beloved, is explicitly placed on the horizon of the poem. Both the woman, symbolized by the letter that is pronounced like her first name and by the country that gives her her last name, and the song, designated by its refrain, which echoes the poet's feelings, are the object of his love and the source of his inspiration. Just as the letter designates and dissimulates the loved woman, the song serves as a go-between for the expression of love. The poet turns it to his own account while at the same time holding it at a distance, within quotation marks. He explains that he does not sing it—"La chanson est (sans en dire le son)"—a way of saying that its destiny is to be sung and that he does violence to it by inserting it into a poem that is not made to be sung. And he points out the contrast; he reveals its meaning at the end of the epigram: "Elle se chante à la vieille façon / Mais c'est tout ung, la brunette est jeunette."

For the love of a young lady, he loves an old song. He loves it for being a song, but he does not sing it. "Elle se chante à la vieille façon," it is sung in the old fashion, but it inspires him with a new poem. Everything is calculated to bring out the effect of contrast and of quotation which I briefly analyzed—without great merit, since it goes without saying—regarding the *khardjas*. The flavor of the epigram comes from the fact that it is grounded in the reminiscence of an old and simple song and from the fact that it uses its subtlety, its ingenuity, to foreground the artless confession of love and of suffering. An old and simple song: Everything, in that single line, designates it as such: *alléger* used as an absolute verb to mean "alléger les peines de l'amour," "to relieve the pains of love"; *douce* as an expression of affection, which is found constantly during the Middle Ages in the most common formulae of civility among children and in decent society ("belle douce amie," "belle douce soeur," beautiful sweet friend, beautiful sweet sister); the invariable form of the epicene adjective *plaisant*, already a bit obsolete in the sixteenth century; and the expression "plaisant brunette," which one already finds in a little dance rondeau from the thirteenth century. And even the fact that the woman is a brunette, which is to say, a popular beauty (Anne d'Alençon was probably dark, though there was nothing popular about her beauty, and the touching aspect of the indirect quotation and of its new use is increased by that fact). Youth and old age, novelty and antiquity, sophistication and rusticity stand opposed and then come together, bring each other into relief. The poet waxes sentimental about his old song, but he is not its dupe, and he lets that be known. To love an outmoded and simplistic song is all very well, if it is at a remove, for the benefit of a young love and a fashionable epigram.

So much for the two instances of quotation and the two uses Marot made of the same song. Nothing much. Do we have to give so much weight to such minuscule details? And yet, is it truly insignificant to see this poet becoming aware that the song he loves is not loved solely because he feels close to it, in agreement with its sentiments but also, but especially, because, however close it may be, it is also far away from him, because it is an old song, because it gives a rudimentary and stiff expression to his feelings? Is it insignificant to see the poet draw the consequences of that fact in the order of his art, seeking first to assimilate that song to the norms of poetry, since he loves it and sees himself in it, then to ground his poetry in the contrast that opposes it to that song, since he loves it and sees himself in it from a distance? Is it a matter of indifference to see him, from one poem to the next, making this song into an old song?

Marot was still largely a medieval poet and the son of a *grand rhétoriqueur*. But he is also traditionally presented as the first great poet of the Renaissance. That is the point of view I would seem to be adopting here, since it is with him that I begin the descent toward modern times, down to romanticism, before heading back to the Middle Ages, and since I seem to be discerning in him an evolution that could only distance him from his origins. But in the Middle Ages we will again find, in an almost habitual manner, the effect of which he shows such an acute awareness and which he exploits with such refinement in his epigram. It is therefore not absurd to begin with him and the songs as a way of illustrating the thesis that the modern age uses the medieval literary past in a way that was suggested to it by medieval literature itself.

The taste shown by Alceste and Saint-Preux in the matter of songs shows that they are also sensitive to this kind of effect: "old song," "old romances," "something ancient and sweet about them," "the rhyme is not rich and the style is old," "[the] tunes are not captivating," "the words are simple and naive." Must we confine ourselves to saluting that lovely continuity? It does not go without saying, however, at least not to the degree one might think. For the notion of antiquity associated with song, a notion whose implicit and latent presence in the quotation from Montaigne I had so much trouble indicating, is constantly opposed to a different notion, that of novelty. Among the 180 songs enumerated in chapter 33 bis of Rabelais's *Cinquième Livre*, at the feast Pantagruel attends in the kingdom of the Lanternois, one discerns very ancient songs, rustic in coloration but also and especially fashionable tunes, sentimental songs, bawdy songs. More exactly, one discerns that all these songs are cited only because they are on everyone's lips and are known by all. We will see later on that the confrontation between antiquity and novelty is, in a fairly complex way, at the heart of medieval lyric effects. But also— and that is why this remark is made about Molière and Rousseau— one might think that, precisely in the seventeenth and eighteenth centuries, novelty ought to prevail. For although a few songs that have survived to the modern era go back to the fifteenth century, or even a bit further, the immense majority of the pieces traditionally designated as French "popular songs" appeared in the seventeenth or eighteenth century. We first learn of these songs from printed collections, brochures peddled in the streets, loose sheets sold in Paris. We learn of them first as fashionable songs.

Just as the peasant costumes of the regions of France generally reproduce the fashions of that era and seem to have become fixed at that time, so is it with French popular songs. That at least is what the most attentive and most scholarly research reveals. But once more, the impression that belies the positive demonstration conceals a share of truth in its own right. The impression was that of contemporaries, of Molière and Rousseau. It was perhaps already that of Malherbe, who, if we are to believe Tallemant des Réaux, affected a preference for *D'où venez-vous, Jeanne? / Jeanne, d'où venez?* (Where do you come from, Jeanne, / Jeanne, where are you from?) and *Que me donnerez-vous? Je ferai l'endormie* (What will you give me? / I'll pretend to be asleep) over the poems of Ronsard. In the eighteenth century, it was the impression of the first collectors of popular songs, such as Christophe Ballard. For them, and for us as well perhaps, simple and artless songs, songs sung among the people, are old songs, are at every moment old songs. The people are eternal youth and eternal great age. Tales and songs are always supposed to belong to the next to last generation and to pass from the grandmothers to the grandchildren, skipping the flat coincidence with the present which makes middle age so drab. They are like Sleeping Beauty, who, in the freshness of her fifteenth year, has "a high collar as our grandmothers used to wear." Thus she captures the prince's heart. They are like Nerval's Sylvie in her old aunt's wedding gown: "Oh! I shall look like an old fairy!—'The fairy of legend, eternally young,' I said to myself."[17] They are like the young man in "the gamekeeper's uniform of the house of Condé," forever young in his gilded frame but whose garb and haircut, dating from the *ancien régime* (not so long ago, in fact), leave us on the banks of the dead, beyond the chasm of history.

Yes, the songs are like Sylvie, fresh and young in that charming, yellowed, and out-of-style wedding gown, offering to the blank gaze of the portrait, the tired gaze of the aunt, the avid and timid gaze of her "beloved," the living present full of the promise of an irremediably lost past. And the aunt, in seeing her, "rediscovers in her memory the alternating songs in vogue at the time . . . and the naive epithalamium." The two young people "repeat these stanzas with their simple rhythm, with the hiatus and assonances of the time."[18] The songs are like Adrienne, the distant and grave little girl, more alive than all the living beings in this childhood memory that shaped a life—but lost forever, deader than all the dead. The confirmation of her death closes the narrative ("Poor Adrienne! She died in the convent of Saint-S—— in about 1832").[19] Adrienne, who made her song expressive by imitating the voice of a grandmother: "The melody ended each stanza with those quavering trills that young voices stress so well, when they imitate with a modulated tremor the trembling voices of grandmothers."[20]

Her song was an old song: "She sang one of those old romances full of melancholy and love, which always tell of the misfortunes of a princess closed up in her tower by the will of a father, who punishes her for having loved."

To all appearances, her song was *Le roi Loÿs est sur son pont* (King Louis is on his bridge), Gérard de Nerval's favorite song, and the one that haunted her "from cradle to grave."

This is not really my fault. How could anyone talk of songs without referring to Nerval? Who better than he understood that songs have to do with the past, with old age, and with childhood, with his own childhood? But what is there to add on this theme to the wonderful book by Paul Bénichou, *Nerval et la chanson folklorique* (Nerval and the folkloric song)?[21]

Nerval continued to reuse his own texts (and sometimes those of others, in fact) and, before the invention of word processing, to practice "cut and paste." His writings on songs, the excursus he devotes to them and the use he makes of them in his short stories, his essays, his various literary rambles, need to be followed, reassembled, compared. The same developments come back, often identical for pages on end except for a word or two but each time differently colored by the context, in his articles, in *Les faux-saulniers*, in *La bohême galante*, in *Angélique*, in *Sylvie*, and elsewhere. There as everywhere in Nerval, the movement from the first to the last texts is that of a progressive internalization, a kind of integration of his material into the strata of the self. The oldest text—not the most interesting but one of the most complete and the most structured—his article *Les vieilles ballades françaises* (The old French ballads), published in *La Sylphide* on 10 July 1842, opens with considerations characteristic of romantic thought, without great originality, on the antiquity of oral productions and the national interest there would be in gathering together the "French *romancero*." These considerations are formulated in terms so close to those used ten years later by Paulin Paris in requesting the creation of a chair of language and literature in medieval French at the Collège de France that we might wonder whether P. Paris did not remember the article. As it happens, Nerval spoke of Paulin Paris on several occasions and, in *La main enchantée* (The enchanted hand), praised his kindness and competence in carrying out his duties as manuscript curator at the Bibliothèque Royale. Let us return to that article and cite its first lines: "Before they wrote, every people sang; all poetry is inspired by its naive sources, and Spain, Germany, and England each cite with pride their national romancero. Why does not France have its own?"[22]

The rest of the article is devoted for the most part to metrical considerations, a pretext for long quotations, which delighted Nerval. He sees the irregular versification of popular French songs as the reason they were held in disdain. It is not certain that he always analyzes accurately that supposed irregularity.[23] But for him, it is the mark of the people and of the past. That is what holds his interest in these songs and endlessly leads him back to them: the trace of history and of his childhood, erudition and memory, the loves of Angélique and the voice of Adrienne, the paths of the Valois tirelessly trod, his little canton of memory.

For it is all a matter of memory. Should he happen to dig into the archives (J. Guillaume and C. Pichois have shown he actually did so) and exhume the life of Angélique de Longueval? Then the beautiful girl's love affairs, thwarted by her father's strictness, bring to his mind and his writing (or more precisely, lead him to draw from the stock of developments exploited since the article in *La Sylphide*) the song *Le roi Loÿs est sur son pont*, called forth by an offhand transition: "As for the character of fathers in the province I am traveling through, it has always been the same, if I am to believe the legends I heard sung in my youth. It is a mixture of coarseness and good-heartedness that is altogether patriarchal. Here is one of the songs I was able to collect from the old region of Ile-de-France."[24]

After he has quoted the song almost in its entirety, an even more offhand transition leads to commentary on and excerpts from the song *Dessous le rosier blanc / La belle se promène* (Beneath the white rosebush / The beauty takes a walk): "We have just seen the ferocious father; here now is the indulgent father."

"The province I am traveling through"; "one of the songs I was able to collect from that old region of Ile-de-France": The song is a relic of that province's past, and it bears witness to the "patriarchal" mores of yesteryear. But its appeal is that it belongs to the narrator's past, to the paths traveled, to the legends heard, to his own roots in that province. Without being too much a dupe to that distortion, Nerval has a tendency to present songs widespread in numerous regions as proper to the Valois. Having happened upon the story of Angélique de Longueval while seeking that of Abbot de Bucquoy, only too happy to find in it a pretext to go searching near Senlis, he is directed from library archives to the archives of memory. Leaving the cathedral of Senlis after the services on All Souls' Day, he happens upon a group of little girls singing old songs:

> And the little girl began to sing in a weak but sonorous voice: "Les canards dans la rivière . . . etc." (The ducks in the river etc.).
>
> Yet another tune that soothed me as a child. Childhood memories are revived when one reaches the midpoint of life. It is like a palimpsest manuscript whose lines are made to reappear by chemical processes.
>
> Together, the little girls began another song—again a memory:
>
> Trois filles dedans un pré . . .
> Mon coeur vole [bis]!
> Mon coeur vole à mon gré!
>
> Three girls in a meadow . . .
> My heart flies [bis]
> My heart flies at will![25]

All Souls' Day, the midpoint of life, childhood memories, the spectacle of childhood, memory effaced and brought back to life as in a palimpsest: The final comparison confirms the link between the world of writing—of archives—and that of reminiscence, of personal memory, and of orality. All the elements that link song to the past, to memory, to rustic childhood, and to its simplicity are present here.

And all these elements are explicitly brought together again in the first sentence of *Chansons et légendes du Valois*, that postscript of sorts added to *Sylvie*, as if these songs and legends of the Valois revealed the ultimate secret of that transparent and mysterious book: "Each time my thought turns to the memories of that province of the Valois, I recall with delight the songs and stories that soothed me in my childhood. . . . Today I cannot manage to complete them, for everything is profoundly forgotten; the secret dwells in the tombs of grandmothers."[26]

After such a personal beginning, Nerval once more argues for the return to a poetry at once popular and national, the poetry of French songs. Certain of them have the value of "a Uhland ballad."[27]

Is it therefore true poetry, is it the melancholic thirst for the ideal that this people lack, for them to understand and produce songs worthy of being compared to those of Germany and England? Certainly not; but it happened that in France literature never descended to the level of the great mob; the academic poets of the seventeenth and eighteenth centuries would have no more understood such inspirations than the peasants would have admired their odes, their epistles, and their fleeting poems, so colorless, so stiff. Yet let us again compare the song I shall cite to all these bouquets to Chloris, which around that time were so admired in the best society. [Nerval then cites *Quand Jean Renaud de la guerre revint* (When Jean Renaud came back from the war)].[28]

During the same period or shortly before, the application of a notion of this kind, based on popular songs or rather on the confusion between medieval poetry and popular songs, led scholars and poets back to the Middle Ages. That is our true object, to which I come finally, after indulging in far too many detours.

These detours are unjustifiable. If I were to attempt to justify them, however, I would say that no one better than Nerval gives us to understand that the antiquity of songs is perceived only when transposed onto the recesses of memory, and the recesses of memory onto the feeling of loss and forgetting. We—that is, he, Gérard, and each of us who reads him—we cite only bits of these songs. We are distressed that we cannot reproduce the tunes. We have forgotten them. We have abandoned the land of our childhood, we do not recognize our foster brother, we have neglected Sylvie, lost Sylvie, we have let the sole chance to possess her slip us by. Thus, "the fairy of legend, eternally young" no longer sings the old songs:

"So sing me the song of the pretty girl abducted from her father's garden, from under the white rosebush."
"No one sings that any more."
"Might you have become a musician?"
"Somewhat."
"Sylvie, Sylvie, I am sure you sing operatic arias!"
"Why are you complaining?"
"Because I loved the old tunes, and you will no longer know how to sing them."
Sylvie modulated a few sounds from a great modern operatic aria. . . . She *was phrasing.*[29]

And later, but too late:

"Are you lost in reflection?" said Sylvie, and she began to sing:

A Dammartin l'y a trois belles filles:
L'y en a z'une plus belle que le jour . . .

In Dammartin are three pretty girls:
And one of them is prettier than day . . .

"Ah! You wicked thing!" I cried: "You see very well you still know old songs."
"If you were to come here more often, I would remember them."[30]

The entire lesson of *Sylvie* is that reality exists only in memory.[31] But how is that lesson given? What marks memory as memory, what signals that what is present to consciousness is from the past, is song. The lesson of *Sylvie* lies in the songs and legends of the Valois, which are its curious and necessary continuation and conclusion.

For the songs that come back to memory in bits and pieces, half effaced, half forgotten, are designated as remnants emerging from the past by that oblivion itself, by their link to rustic mores that city fashions threaten to efface. That is because they belong to great age—to the grandmothers—and to childhood, to our own forever vanished childhood. In a childhood memory as inaccessible and as present to consciousness as a dream—the memory of an evening party—a little girl close enough to kiss, a little girl whose image will haunt for a lifetime, a little girl inaccessible because she belonged to another milieu, because she disappeared, because she entered a convent, because she died, a little girl fleetingly perceived in another world and gone to the next world, sang an old song, making her fresh voice quaver as if it were the voice of an old woman.

And what about the Middle Ages in all that? They seem forgotten, and yet they are close at hand. For romanticism, for the heirs of Vico and Herder, for their translators Michelet and Quinet, for the first philologists, the Middle Ages, which are very old, are the world of our ancestors, but they are also the poetic youth of our civilization. They are very far away, but they conceal a truth about ourselves so close and burning that it brings the color to our cheeks. That truth is hidden in our childhood and revealed by it. And the Middle Ages too mark their proximity and their distance through their songs, which are the first manifestations of their—of our—literary art. The first moment of medieval studies, which we shall now examine in less evanescent fashion, consisted in assuming a continuity between the songs of the Middle Ages, which soothed the poetic childhood of the peoples from whom we came, and the songs that in our own time soothed us in our childhood and which seem to emanate from the memory of the people. When that continuity proved to be essentially illusory, the distress and near total confusion of sensibilities were greater than positive philology, in its apparent coolness, let on.

In the meantime, the final word belongs provisionally to Goethe, who formulated it long ago. In 1806, in his review of *Das Knabenwunderhorn* (The little boy's enchanted horn), he observed "that a man arrived at a certain level of culture finds in popular songs a charm comparable to that of the spectacle of youth or of its memory."[32]

Popular Songs and Medieval Songs

Where Are the People?

At the very moment when Nerval was giving such an affective and aesthetic charge to the songs of the Valois, the interest in popular songs was taking a systematic and scientific turn. In addition, the idea of a continuity between songs of the Middle Ages and popular songs was being shattered, or at the very least, profoundly modified by the effect of a more profound and more rigorous knowledge of both. That evolution appears clearly in the preliminary instructions to the Fortoul survey, which was compiled by Ampère in 1852–53. We find at that time the end of a certain type of confusion between the medieval and the popular, which had reigned since preromanticism. Folklore studies were given a new orientation, and medieval studies as well.

What is the Fortoul survey?

On 13 September 1852, a decree by Louis-Napoléon, based on the report of Minister of Public Education Hippolyte Fortoul, . . . ordered the formation of a *Recueil des poésies populaires de la France* [Collection of popular poems of France] and entrusted its publication to a commission including, among others, J.-J. Ampère,

Saint-Beuve, Nisard, and Mérimée. The first volume of the *Bulletin du comité de la langue, de l'histoire et des arts de la France* [Bulletin of the committee of the language, history, and arts of France, for 1852–53], which appeared only in 1854, contained the *Instructions du Comité* [Instructions of the committee], compiled by Ampère and intended for local collectors.[1]

In short, the Fortoul survey carried out an initiative similar to that launched in 1807 by the young Académie Celtique and relaunched periodically ever since, for example, in 1845 on the initiative of Minister Salvandy, of whom we shall speak later on.

Let us observe, first, that the launching of the Fortoul survey and the creation of a chair of medieval French language and literature at the Collège de France—the first chair dedicated to that discipline in French higher education—occurred simultaneously. The letter from Paulin Paris requesting that the prince-president create such a chair "either at the Collège de France or at the Sorbonne" dates from 20 March 1852, the decree for the Fortoul survey from 13 September. The chair at the Collège de France was created in 1853, the year Ampère compiled the instructions relating to the survey and the year he was himself named professor at the Collège de France. The concerns were parallel: France was lagging behind the other countries of Europe in the study of its literary past and of its popular poetry, and both measures were meant to correct that. In the case of medieval studies, let us recall the terms of the letter from Paulin Paris, which I cited in my inaugural lecture. The same idea was taken up again at the beginning of his own inaugural lecture, delivered on 1 March 1853:

> [In asking that this chair be created] I maintain . . . that the first literature emerging from the shadows that separated us from Roman civilization, and that, as such, offered us the first poems sung and recited, the first romances, and the first dramatic plays, ought to have a distinct place in public education, rather than remaining less well known, less esteemed in France than in the rest of Europe.[2]

In the case of folklore studies, Ampère similarly observed that "France is less advanced" than other countries, but he was full of hope that it would make up for the delay.[3]

These similar concerns, however, did not prevent the two orders of study from having a new awareness of their differences. In his instructions, Ampère is anxious to avoid the confusion, so widespread at the time, between the popular and the medieval and to make clear that the songs of the Middle Ages have no place in a collection of popular songs.[4] The chansons de geste, he explains, lie beyond the domain of the survey, unless "new poems of this kind were to be discovered in their primitive state and obviously bearing the imprint of a truly popular origin."[5] In the same way, "the lyric poems of the troubadours and trouvères ought in general to be excluded, because they are a product of art."[6] These considerations, of course, raise a number of questions. They do not rule out the existence of popular epic poems, within the perspective of a belief in a primitive and national epic. If the chansons de geste do not enter into such a definition, it is less in themselves than because the tradition is no longer living: It would be different if "*new* poems" of this kind were to be found. The underlying idea is that authentically popular literature combines an ancient tradition and continual renewal. On the other hand, the exclusion of the troubadours and trouvères for the excellent and irrefutable reason that their poems are "a product of art" implies that there is a "purely natural" popular poetry, as Montaigne would have said, which is less self-evident.

In a word, the poetry of the Middles Ages is in great part learned, and the tradition is no longer living: two reasons to exclude it from a collection of popular songs. That is also the feeling of Nerval, who, before he could read the instructions drafted by Ampère, suspected the Fortoul survey a priori of attempting to compile medieval texts in an erudite manner rather than collect old French songs in the field.[7]

This opposition between medieval literature and popular literature ran counter to a movement that had been developing for more than half a century. And it compelled medievalists to reflect anew on the notion of popular literature when applied to the Middle Ages. Let us take a look at the situation before and after that moment, which I have signaled by an event more noteworthy for its emblematic value than for its real consequences, for in actuality the Fortoul survey fell short of its aim.

Beginning in the middle of the eighteenth century, a romance genre in the troubadour style had developed in France. Its most characteristic practitioner was F.-A. P. de Moncrif (*La comtesse de Saulx*), who was imitated by Pierre-Antoine de La Place (*Le comte Orry*), by Berquin, by Duke de La Vallière (*Les infortunées amours de Cominge, Les infortunées amours de Gabrielle de Vergi et de Raoul de Couci*),[8] by Cazotte (*La veillée de la bonne femme ou le réveil d'Enguerrand* and *Les prouesses inimitables d'Olliver, marquis d'Edesse*, cited and commented on by Nerval in *Les illuminés*), and by others. The word *romance* was borrowed from the Spanish (*romances, romancero*), where, since the Middle Ages, it had designated narrative poems conserved in part by the oral tradition; it was introduced into French with this meaning in the sixteenth century. It was preferred to the term *ballade*, used in a similar sense in Germanic countries, because of the confusion with the well-known fixed-form genre of French lyricism that originated in the fourteenth century. The romances combined two traits. First, they were situated by choice in the Middle Ages. Second, though they were not in the least popular, they claimed to have their roots in popular inspiration: They picked up traditional tunes and fragments and cultivated a naive and simple style, whose artifice was extreme but was for that reason only the more revealing of an aesthetic choice. They thus associated the medieval with the popular.

That association occurred in England and Germany at the same time, but in a different spirit that proved more productive. In fact, French romance writers were not deeply interested either in the medieval past or in popular traditions. They did not seek to truly know them. All they asked from them was a superficial coloration, to produce the effect of touching naivete. In England and in Germany, in contrast, beginning with the second half of the eighteenth century, the interest in popular songs and in the medieval memories whose traces they might conceal was real and, we might say, serious. Two remarks on that adjective, which I do not use by chance. On one hand, the lack of seriousness of the French spirit was a reproach made constantly by other nations. In the case of songs, the first German scholars stemming from romanticism judged that frivolous and fickle tastes in France were harmful to the preservation of popular songs. Here are the words of O. L. B. Wolff, from his *Altfranzösische Lieder* (note that he speaks of "popular songs" regarding songs in Old French), published in Leipzig in 1831:

> No people are so rich in songs as the French, none are so poor in popular songs. That has to do with their character: provided they are singing, they are satisfied, what they sing is a matter of indifference to them, provided it interests them, and that interest is purely ephemeral.[9]

But on the other hand, can one really call serious the interest in England and Germany at the time, directed toward popular literature and its possible roots in the Middle Ages? The poetry of Ossian was an acknowledged fake. Arnim and Brentano's *Das Knabenwunderhorn* sparked a polemic regarding its authenticity upon its publication. Ernest Tonnelat has shown that the Brothers Grimm did much more rewriting than they admitted of the tales they claimed were transcribed as they had collected them from the lips of their informer.[10] But that is not a question of seriousness. It is a matter of presuppositions and of literary, ethnographic, aesthetic, and even ethical choices, to which we will soon have occasion to return.

It is nonetheless true that, while Moncrif was composing *Les infortunes inouïes de la tant belle, tant honnête et renommée comtesse de Saulx* (1751; The unheard-of misfortunes of the so beautiful, so honest and renowned countess of Saulx), in Northamptonshire the Anglican pastor Thomas Percy was collecting the pieces for his *Reliques of English Poetry*, which he published in 1765. In fact, Percy—who, according to Burke, was himself a bit of a snob[11]—did not think the ballads he was collecting, and whose antiquity he underscored in the archaic French spelling of "reliques," had originated among the people. On the contrary, he believed they were composed by minstrels and intended for the court. In the 1760s as well, the Scotsman James

Macpherson "translated" the poems of Ossian (Oisin Mac Finn, a Welsh bard who supposedly lived during the third century), eliciting enthusiasm throughout Europe, from Herder to Goethe, from Napoleon to Chateaubriand. Chateaubriand even became his French translator. We shall see in a moment the influence of the Ossianic poems on Claude Fauriel, one of the French medievalists, who devoted a great deal of his effort to the study of popular poems throughout Europe. Then came Herder.[12] His ideas on popular poetry had already been outlined in his *Fragmente zur deutschen Literatur* (Fragments on German literature) in 1767. In 1773, he gave a more developed expression to these ideas in his essay *Über Ossian und die Lieder alter Völker* (On Ossian and the songs of ancient peoples), published in the collection *Blätter von deutscher Art und Kunst* (Pages on German art). In 1778 the collection of *Volkslieder* appeared—later reprinted under the title *Stimmen der Völker in Liedern* (The voice of the people in song)—and the essay *Über die Wirkung der Dichtkunst auf die Sitten der Völker* (The effect of the poetic arts on the mores of peoples).

Herder secured the success of the term and notion of *Volkslied*, a notion that was clarified by A. W. Schlegel in a course given in Berlin in 1803–4. In my inaugural lecture, I recalled in very summary fashion the link between the poetry of the Middle Ages and popular poetry in Herder's hypothesis, which is that the collective, national, and primitive identity of the peoples of Europe is revealed through both. But this link also stems from the idea that the *Volkslied* expresses the youth of a people and of their language. Allow me to cite at length J.-A. Bizet, who gives an excellent summary of Herder's conceptions:

> For him, young peoples speak a young language, full in its sonority, vigorous in rhyme; they express themselves in images that are already poems in germ; they excel at seizing the individual note, in making the characteristic trait salient. Objects in popular poetry take on a clear and precise outline that takes root in the imagination because of its plasticity. No reflection intervenes between the impression felt and its poetic rendering: the expression corresponds to an intense sensation and a true feeling. . . .

The poetry of primitive times—or that of peoples who have barely budged from the primitive state, the *Naturzustand*—is in fact not the work of artists conscious of the resources of their craft or simply applied to their task: it is an anonymous work, imputable to the collectivity within which it came to life; that is as much to say that it is made by a work of the collective unconscious. For that reason it faithfully expresses natural genius, the *Naturgeist* of the ethnic group from which it emanates. . . .

When peoples reach adulthood, the virile stage after childhood, writers succeed poets, the language of songs (*die Liedersprache*) gives way to that of books (*Büchersprache*); a poetry of art—*eine Kunstpoesie* (note that the word also means "artificial poetry")—develops on the ruins of natural poetry, *Naturpoesie*.[13]

In short, as I already underscored, Herder found common ground with Vico. Also significant of their influence in France is the fact that Herder was translated by Quinet in 1828 and Vico by Michelet in 1827 and 1835. And in 1828, at the very time he was occupied with Vico, Michelet was also planning to publish a collection of French songs.[14] The idea of nature and the metaphor of youth thus continued to be intertwined and, at the same time, to call for the association between medieval and popular poetry.

This is evident in the impact Herder's ideas were soon to have in Germany among the young poets. The very title of the famous collection of popular German songs published in 1806 by Achim von Arnim and Clemens Brentano, *Das Knabenwunderhorn*, was a reference to the Middle Ages, since the enchanted horn in question was that of *Le lai du cor*.[15] Yet the Middle Ages are invoked by means of a detour through a French romance, depicted in the original illustration for the title page. Brentano in particular was sensitive to the untimeliness of the *Volkslied* and its ancient roots, which made for its charm and value. Arnim, it is true, having celebrated a Germania immersed in its medieval past in his essay *Von Volksliedern*, dreamt for his part of making the *Volkslied* a very timely political instrument, directed against the ideology of enlightenment introduced into Germany by Napoleon's conquests.

But the association between popular song and medieval poetry took a more systematic and more critical turn with Ludwig Uhland. He discovered popular song through the *Wunderhorn* and also read Herder's *Stimmen der Völker* and Percy's *Reliques*. His own poetry deliberately and effectively took on a popular and discreetly archaic coloration, to the point of almost dissolving into folklore at times, as for example in *Der Wirtin Töcheterlein* (The hostess's daughter) or *Der gute Kamerad* (The good comrade). This last piece, sung to a traditional tune, went on to know the fortune familiar to us. This archaism came to shore up a disconcerting, but in reality rather profound, remark later made by Weckerlin, who compared French and German songs:

> In France, there are three different sorts of song: 1) the popular song; 2) the city song (court carols, topical songs); and 3) the art song.
>
> Like us, the Germans have the first and third categories, but as for their second, it differs essentially from ours, since they have a *popular form* [*volksthümlich*] song,[16] that is, a song the poet models on the popular form, and which the people generally adopt without knowing the author's name. We must not confuse this sort of song with our *turlutaines* from the cabarets, which the people bawl out along the boulevards; no, these are true popular songs in their content, but with a more correct form than that of the ancient songs, and are often also more musical than they.[17]

It is true that in Germany there was never any hesitation in associating, or even combining, popular songs and songs of "popular form," as Weckerlin says. The pieces Herder placed among his *Volkslieder* demonstrated this at the end of the eighteenth century, as did the composition of the *Kommersbuch* by German students at the end of the nineteenth. The *Kommersbuch* was a collection of songs, destined to accompany feasts and drinking sessions and containing popular songs, poems by known authors put to music, patriotic songs, and so on. During that era, some authors corrected the romantic idea of collective creation by maintaining that although the popular song certainly represents the unanimity of the people, it is an individual creation. That is the position of Franz Böhme in his *Altdeutsches Liederbuch*.[18]

But Uhland's originality did not really lie in that aptitude for composing "popular form" songs. Brentano and Heine did the same: Think of the two *Loreleis*, Brentano's, which Apollinaire adapted, and Heine's, which became such a popular song that the Nazis were unable to ban it from the manuals and had to be content with claiming—the supreme tribute—that it was anonymous.[19] What was unique to Uhland was that he studied German and French medieval literature with the zeal of the scholar. In 1810, he spent long months in Paris, where he read chansons de geste and poems by the troubadours at the Bibliothèque Impériale. He produced an essay based on his research, *Über das altfranzösische Epos* (The Old French epic), and many of the works in his *Balladen und Romanzen* (Ballads and romances) draw on that inspiration: *Bertrand de Born*, the name of a famous troubadour; *Merlin der Wilde* (Merlin the Wild); *Klein Roland* (The young Roland); *Roland Schildträger* (Squire Roland); *König Karls Meerfahrt* (The sea voyage of King Charles); *Taillefer*, the name of a jongleur supposed to have sung *La chanson de Roland* at the beginning of the Battle of Hastings; and others. When he returned to the *Volkslieder* much later, at the end of long preparatory labor on manuscript and printed sources, his application, erudition, and a certain cool judgment that was the exact opposite of the subjective enthusiasm of romanticism, plus his real knowledge of medieval literature, made his views penetrating and in great part new. He expressed them in 1830 in his *Geschichte der altdeutschen Poesie* (History of Old German poetry), fifteen years later in his *Abhandlung über die deutschen Volkslieder* (Essay on popular German songs), which remained uncompleted, and in the conception of *Alte hoch- und niederdeutsche Volkslieder* (Old popular songs in High and Low German), a collection published in two volumes in 1844 and 1845.

In the particular case of the relation between popular and medieval poetry, Uhland maintained that popular poetry had in a sense been snuffed out by the aristocratic and refined poetry of the *Minnesänger*, which had initially fed on it (he confines himself to the German field, but his analyses would have the same value for Romance poetry). The decline of the *Minnesang* brought about a kind of resurgence of the popular vein: The most ancient popular songs we know of would thus go back to the fourteenth and fifteenth centuries. In other words, he shored up and argued, in a manner that would be shared by most medievalists, the theory that led Ampère a few years later to exclude the songs of the Middle Ages from the Fortoul survey.

In addition, Uhland considerably nuanced the romantic belief in a collective creation. He showed the share attributable to the author, even unknown, and the conditions under which the songs were transformed and deformed. He considered their incoherencies, disjointedness, and abruptness to be merely corruptions in transmission, whereas the romantics, like Herder (and even the *Stürmer und Dränger*, the German preromantics), had discerned them as an aesthetic trait of the *Volkslied*. On that last point, as you may have guessed, I agree with the romantics. For if these characteristics had not been pleasing in themselves, the songs would have been reconstituted as they were corrupted, as was the case during the Middle Ages in certain areas of literary transmission. Nonetheless, Uhland was the first to attempt, through precise and scholarly argument, to account for what Patrice Coirault has called the "formation of our folkloric songs."[20] That concern is again found in the instructions to the Fortoul survey, which insist on the need to collect scrupulously the variants of each song.

But all the same, the leap from Ludwig Uhland to Hippolyte Fortoul seems abrupt, whatever mediation there might have been between Germany and France in the romantic age, in particular through Heine and Nerval, and before that, through Mme de Staël. We must not believe that Germany had the monopoly for all those years on reflections regarding the relation between popular and medieval songs, or that France simply continued its affectation of the troubadour style, or even that the conception of a "poetic childhood of peoples," inherited from Vico and Herder, was applied without reflection or nuance to medieval literature in France. Uhland's position, applied to the Romance field and developed with firm precision by Friedrich Diez (*Altromanische Sprachdenkmale*—Ancient monuments of the Romance languages),[21] was in reality close to the position reached by Fauriel, who was also a great connoisseur and admirer of German literature.

It is, of course, ridiculous to have to mention in a few words the considerable contribution of Claude Fauriel (1772–1844) to the question that concerns us here. It is not that he had an accurate vision of the literature of the Middle Ages, and in particular of Occitan literature, in which he was especially interested. Already in 1889, Alfred Jeanroy's thesis *Les origines de la poésie lyrique en France au Moyen Age* (The origins of lyric poetry in medieval France) challenged most of his views.[22] And it is not that, on the points on which he was right, he was the only one to be right: During the same period, we find similar formulations in Diez and Wackernagel. But the heart of his concerns, the conjunction between the popular songs of Europe as a whole and of medieval literature, can only hold our attention. His influence on the literary milieus of his time was considerable. Finally, we would like to linger over the fate of that child of the Enlightenment, who become a kind of theorist of romanticism, the polyglot scholar with a thousand interests, whose early life, before he turned into a university professor and member of the Institut, was rather adventurous and Stendhalian.

He began life as a humble provincial from Saint-Etienne, born to a joiner father (almost like the sawmill of the elder Sorel in Stendhal's *Le rouge et le noir*—The red and the black) and to a mother who died giving birth to him. He studied with the Oratorians, which ought to have led him to the priesthood, and got caught up in the tumult of the Revolution in the provinces by one of his friends, an unfrocked priest who became "secretary of war." He occupied a succession of posts of all sorts, from which he quickly resigned, was employed in Le Puy in 1793, served as second lieutenant in the Mountain Legion, was municipal officer in his native town, and in 1795 became a student as part of the first and short-lived class of the Ecole Normale. Threatened upon his return to Saint-Etienne by the royalist reaction, he was hired by the administration charged with outfitting the army of the Alps. He again became secretary-general for the commune of Saint-Etienne, then national secretary (procurator) at the civil tribunal of that city. He then moved to Paris, was hired by the ministry of the police, and served as private secretary to Fouché from 1799 to 1802, resigning a few months after the coup d'état of 18 Brumaire. From that year on, he lived with Condorcet's widow, until her death twenty years later; he was very close to Mme de Staël and was associated with all the literary personalities of France, Germany, and Italy. In particular, he was the intimate friend of Manzoni.[23]

In 1793, the young Fauriel read Ossian with passion. Ten years later, his first critical studies focused on Sanskrit—which he learned along with so many other languages—on Raynouard's *Choix des poésies originales des troubadours* (Selection of original poems by the troubadours), and on Roquefort's edition of Marie de France. In 1824–25, he published his *Chants populaires de la Grèce moderne* (Popular songs of modern Greece), with a preliminary essay devoted to the birth and development of popular song (we find the echo of his *Chants grecs* in Victor Hugo's *Orientales* and of this preliminary essay in the preface to *Odes et ballades*). In 1830, he was named professor at the Faculté des Lettres at the University of Paris, to a chair of foreign literature founded with him in mind, and he made the study of medieval Provençal poetry the core of his teaching. In 1836 he published the four volumes of *Histoire de la Gaule méridionale sous la domination des conquérants germaniques* (The history of southern Gaul under the domination of Germanic conquerors), which earned him entry into the Académie des Inscriptions et Belles-Lettres. His *Histoire de la poésie provençale* (History of Provençal poetry), on which he had been working since 1806, was published posthumously, in three volumes in 1847, thanks to his disciple Mary Clarke and the Orientalist Jules Mohl. As a prelude to his course on Provençal poetry, he engaged in considerations on the general characteristics of epic poetry, focusing on Homeric and Hindu poems and on the *Niebelungenlied*. In 1831–32, he devoted a course to popular Greek and Serbian poems—a course that was published by M. Ibrovac in 1966. Two years later, his course dealt with Dante but was expanded to include popular Italian poetry. It was published twenty years later, in 1854, ten years after his death, again thanks to Jules Mohl and Mary Clarke—who had in the meantime become Mme Jules Mohl—under the title *Dante et les origines de la langue et de la littérature italienne* (Dante and the origins of Italian language and literature). In short, for his entire life, Fauriel juggled the study of popular poetry and that of medieval poetry (an examination of the enormous Fauriel collection at the Bibliothèque de l'Institut de France is particularly instructive in this regard).

Yet for all that, he did not confuse them. In the case of the Middle Ages, he established a distinction similar to Uhland's, the same distinction that then took root among all scholars. The recognition of the learned and aristocratic character of the poetry of the troubadours led them to reevaluate the notion of popular poetry when applied to the Middle Ages. Allow me to cite a long passage from the first pages of *Histoire de la poésie provençale*:

> Another characteristic shared by all the lyric compositions we have considered up to this point is that they were written in the purest Provençal, and with all the resources, all the meticulous care, of the art of the troubadours. As a whole, they constituted a refined and learned poetry that required—that presupposed—practiced and discerning judges. It was a poetry of the courts and castles, not of public squares and streets; a poetry that contained a multitude of things the people could not understand, or in which they could hardly be interested even if they did understand them. Hence, either there was no popular poetry in the South of France or that poetry was different from the ordinary poetry of the troubadours.
>
> The first of these two suppositions is hardly plausible: it is contrary to everything we know about the character and imagination of peoples of the Provençal language, to everything I have said about the beginnings of their literature. In fact, these pious legends, these hymns in the vernacular, which were early on sung in churches and in the streets, these romantic tales of Christian lords in search of adventure among the Saracens; all these were undoubtedly popular in form and content. Finally, it was among the people, and from popular feeling, that the poetry of these regions was born: there is thus no likelihood that in becoming refined in the castles, that poetry abruptly disappeared from the cities.
>
> But, leaving aside the arguments based on plausibility, we can

directly assert that there was in the South of France, in the twelfth and thirteenth centuries, a true popular poetry. That fact will better reveal itself in what follows, but I can at present give a few indications of it. There is some evidence of it in history itself and in the works of the troubadours.

Exhausted by the effort they had to exert to be brilliant in the artificial poetry of the castles, these troubadours, from a kind of instinct related to their talent itself, and which was a proof of it, sometimes returned to nature; and, in these fits of simplicity, they sang for city people and country people. The collections of the best troubadours offer a few of these pieces, which are easily distinguished from all the others. Within the poetic whole to which they belong, they form a particular class that will merit a separate examination.[24]

It is easy—too easy—to find in this passage the traces or expression of all Fauriel's errors. He grants too much to poetry in Provençal—or langue d'oc, as we prefer to say today—seeing it as the cradle not only of lyric poetry but also of the chanson de geste and the romance. Even before Gaston Paris, he believed that chansons de geste derived from cantilenas, were born among the people, and were contemporary to the events whose memory they preserve. Elsewhere, we find him seeking support from the cantilena of Saint Faron, which he, of course, considered an authentic document. He judges the production of romances popular in its inspiration. When we turn to the announced examination of that "particular class" in the production of the troubadours, which appears to him to stem from popular inspiration,[25] we realize that he has grouped together disparate pieces, whose popular character does not leap out: The two songs of Marcabru's *Estornel* stand beside what he calls "ballads," that is, narrative pieces, or beside Guirault de Bornelh's *Reis glorios* (Glorious king) and the French song *Gaite de la tor* (Gaiety of the tower), placed there, it seems, for the sole reason that these are aubades and allow him make a link with Greek songs, κατακοιμητικά, "as someone would say songs of sleep," and διεγερτικά, "songs of awakening."[26]

But that is not the essential thing for us. The essential thing lies in the double movement of Fauriel's thought. The poetry of the troubadours, he tells us, is an intellectually difficult and socially elitist poetry. That is something that everyone during his era was in the process of realizing and which, for their part, Uhland showed regarding the *Minnesänger*, Diez regarding the troubadours themselves. But what he adds is not only that such poetry supplanted a preexisting popular poetry; it is above all that it draws from within itself, that it deliberately secretes, its own popularistic counterpart. Of course, it is less than certain that the troubadours then "sang for the people"—whatever Guirault de Bornelh may have said about "simple folk at the fountain"; it is exactly the reverse. And of course, we might wonder what the "return to nature" means here. But Fauriel has an almost structural vision of a "particular class" within a "poetic whole," a class defined within that whole by an effect of contrast. What he calls "popular genre" does not designate a poetry born of the people or authentically popular but a poetry that uses different effects from its habitual artifice and puts on the appearance of simplicity. In short, Fauriel is not very far from Montaigne's "popular and purely natural poetry," which only the perfection of art allows us to recover once its spontaneity has been lost.

In these early years of the nineteenth century, we thus have three conceptions that are distinguishable from one another but which can also be combined. The first conception sees the poetry of the Middle Ages as an illustration of "the poetic childhood of peoples" and hence a spontaneous emanation of the people. The second recognizes the aristocratic and learned character of the most ancient extant poems but maintains they conceal a more ancient popular poetry, which emerged in the last centuries of the Middle Ages and give birth to the popular songs of the modern era. The third conception—a synchronic view confined to the medieval era—sees "the poetic whole" grounded in a contrasting and simultaneous balance between a difficult poetry and a simple poetry. In my view, as you know, it may be productive to put forward the diachronic permanence, from the Middle Ages to the modern era, of that balance, which exists synchronically at every moment, and also to show that the synchronic balance presupposes a diachronic perception, in the link, or even the assimilation, that is always supposed between simple poetry and ancient poetry.

But let us pause for a moment longer at these three conceptions, since for us they are the occasion to do what we ought perhaps to have done at the beginning but which at the time seemed too abstract and banal. For it is a tired old issue: Watch out for the use of the words *people* and *popular* and for their ambiguity. The word *people* may designate either an ethnic, national identity or a social class, the lowest class, in fact. The first meaning lies at the foundation of the theory of the "poetic childhood of peoples." The second is at work when one observes that the poetry of the Middle Ages is learned and not popular or when one makes an effort to distinguish between a popular culture different from learned culture. Both senses are combined when one opposes a poetry that is both simple and traditional to a poetry both difficult and new, with the implicit idea that the people in the social sense, distanced from progress, from refinement, from the often cosmopolitan innovations in culture and letters, have remained closer to the primitive ethnic identity of the people in the national sense. As late as 1901, the introduction of a short anthology of German *Volkslieder* opened with these words: "The most ancient poetry of a nation is always popular; it is only much later that the poetry of art appears."[27]

More profoundly, as I too briefly recalled in my inaugural lecture, the idea that in going back to the past one moves closer to the people in their primitive authenticity has weighty philosophical and often religious implications for the idea of nature, the theory of an original language, for speculations about the Adamite language and the meaning of the episode of the Tower of Babel,[28] and for the question of the relative proximity of languages and their poetic productions to the Creation as it emerged from the hands of God—their proximity to God himself. We find, for the question that concerns us here, an astonishing example in Wilhelm Wackernagel's introduction to *Altfranzösische Lieder und Leiche aus Handschriften zu Berne und Neuenburg* (Songs and lais in Old French drawn from the Bern and Neuenburg manuscripts; Basel, 1846). For that author, the Romance languages, derived from Latin—and as a result the poetry composed in those languages—are further removed from nature and God, more prey to the arbitrariness of human consciousness and deficiencies, than the Germanic languages, and hence their poetry. According to him, man had no role in the creation of Germanic languages; words were created simultaneously with things. At the same time, however, he recognizes that the work of God manifests itself continuously both in the spontaneity of nature and in human art. That raises to a metaphysical level considerations on the more or less popular character of medieval lyric productions in the various languages. It also considers greater proximity to the primitive and to the original a kind of superiority:

> The Romance languages, born from the ruins of Latin, are a particularly convincing example of the analogy between the acts of nature and those of the human mind, of the fact that God acts and manifests himself equally in one and in the other. . . . But at the same time, since the Romance languages were more prey to the consciousness and arbitrariness of men, how sharply does their human poverty and awkwardness contrast with the force, the richness, the suppleness of the Germanic languages and of all those in whose creation man played no role, whose birth hides a marvelous secret, and whose words were created at the same time as the things they designate.[29]

The ambiguity of the notion of "the people" has led some to reject the expression "popular literature" or "popular songs." Hence, Patrice Coirault observes that in these locutions, "popular" does not signify "in vogue"; rather, with passing time, the "popular song" becomes a song of very limited diffusion:

> "Popular" . . . is no longer a synonym for "in vogue," in fashion among all the people or throughout the country, a meaning well suited to the song of Madelon. Associated with the ancient and with tradition, the word changes in meaning. The tradition of a song can resemble a continuous vogue or fashion. But insofar as it lasts, in becoming extended in time it becomes more restricted in space, and persists only in certain places. The song—disseminated, sporadic—is no longer in vogue or in fashion.[30]

Note the importance of the factors of time, antiquity, tradition. It is they, and not popularity, which make the song popular. Hence Coirault prefers "folkloric" to "popular." But "folkloric" has often seemed laden with unfortunate connotations. Today, one easily speaks of ethnological literature (*ethno-littérature*). But that does not solve the problem, since if we assert that we are considering "the people" only in the ethnic sense of the term and within the perspective of ethnology, we still have to recognize that certain popular productions develop or are conserved in a privileged manner among the people in the social sense of the word. In short, when the situation is viewed synchronically, the word *people* tends to take on its social meaning; when viewed diachronically, it tends to be taken in the ethnic sense.

Thus Herder himself wrote:

Primitive poetry lived in the ears of the people, on the lips of singers. It transmitted history, mysteries, wonders: it was in some way the flower characteristic of peoples, conserving their language, their mores, and initiating future peoples to the mores, passions, sciences, arts, or rather to the occupations of their ancestors.[31]

That is why the noble art of the poet "keeps regenerating itself in the songs of the people, where in fact it had its birth." But he adds, "The people are not those of the streets, who never sing or create, but yell and maim." Here, we already find Weckerlin's disdain for "the *turlutaines* of cabarets," or Coirault's scorn for Madelon. The idealized people, cast back into the past, are carefully distinguished from the contemporary populace. It seems to me that the same disdainful aggressivity is evident among more recent folklorists who, anxious not to be accused of social prejudices, target productions that are not authentically popular, and even more, colleagues who have been misled by such productions. In both cases, violence and disdain actually express the exasperation of never being able to grasp the pure essence of the popular, of seeing it always evaporating, fleeing a bit farther off, a bit deeper into the past, as soon as one believes one holds the object containing it. The acrimony of folklorists (and, for that matter, of medievalists) strengthens my conviction, and even appears to me to be the proof, that the historical reality and the cultural fact they are pursuing, and that they sometimes believe they have grasped, have no objective existence and are nothing more than an aesthetic effect.

For a long time, many have sought the solid foundation that would guarantee the existence of the cultural fact, that is, the continuity and character unique to a popular culture, in historical reality. If the vocation of the "primitive poetry of the people" is to "transmit history," to "conserve the language and mores of peoples" for the use of "future peoples," to paraphrase the passage from Herder cited by Weckerlin and reproduced above, that poetry's roots in history may appear to serve as a criterion of its authenticity and one of its principal interests. That is one of the points that first attracted attention to the poetry of the Middle Ages. In reality, Fauriel has no admiration for chansons de geste and medieval romances (which he still links, let us recall, to the popular vein). But he observes: "These songs or epic materials all belong to ages of ignorance and barbarism, of which they are for us the only documents and whose mores, beliefs, and civilization they faithfully represent. Hence the philosophical and historical interest attached to them."[32]

As for the events themselves, we know that an entire branch of the research believes that traces of the chanson de geste are retained in the memory of the people. But let us remain with the songs supposed to be of the popular tradition. In 1841 L. Le Roux de Lincy published his *Recueil de chants historiques français depuis le XIIe jusqu'au XIVe siècle* (Collection of historical French songs from the twelfth to the fourteenth centuries). "Historical songs": That is his criterion. But it is not that attitude in general that interests me here. It is the effort of certain romantic scholars to find in the popular songs of their time the living memory of events or circumstances dating from the medieval past, and sometimes from the premedieval past. For nowhere is the association between popular poetry and medieval poetry marked—so naively perhaps, but in any case so strongly.

La Villemarqué and the Middle Ages

The example I have chosen and which, I believe, is essential is *Barzaz-Breiz*. First, a brief general reminder about the work and its author and about the enthusiasm and polemics it elicited. Born in Quimperlé, Viscount Théodore Hersart de La Villemarqué (1815–95) came to study in Paris in the 1830s. He took the course of study at the Ecole des Chartes, which provided him with training as a historian and philologist. He was active in liberal Catholic milieus, was particularly close to Montalembert, and frequented Breton milieus in the capital. In 1839, he published *Barzaz-Breiz: Chants populaires de la Bretagne, recueillis et publiés avec une traduction française, des éclairissements, des notes et les mélodies originales* (Barzaz-Breiz: Popular songs of Brittany, collected and published with a French translation, clarifications, notes, and original melodies). It was enormously successful. Chateaubriand and George Sand gave the work an enthusiastic reception and began a warm correspondence with its author. In 1842 La Villemarqué published *Contes populaires des anciens Bretons précédés d'un essai sur l'origine des épopées de la Table Ronde* (Popular tales of the ancient Bretons, preceded by an essay on the origin of the Round Table epics), in 1847 *Essai sur la langue bretonne* (Essay on the Breton language), an introduction to Le Gonidec's *Dictionnaire français-breton et breton-français* (French-Breton and Breton-French dictionary).

Barzaz-Breiz was reissued with additions in 1845 and again in 1867.[33] From that moment on, a polemic developed regarding the authenticity of the collection. Sainte-Beuve had already expressed doubts. In 1872, the folklorist Luzel published a study entitled *De l'authenticité des chants du "Barzaz-Breiz"* (On the authenticity of the songs of "Barzaz-Breiz"), which was very harsh in its conclusions. For Joseph Loth, who was later to occupy the chair of Celtic languages and literatures at the Collège de France, "the old songs [were] pure invention and the language [was] an artificial language." La Villemarqué defended himself only weakly against these accusations, and his silence was taken for a confession. The thesis of a hoax was again defended in 1960 by Francis Gourvil[34] and was even accepted without discussion by Daniel Couty in the *Dictionnaire des littératures de langue française* (Dictionary of literatures of the French language, 1984), which appeared after Donatien Laurent's research, though before the publication of his thesis.

For that research rehabilitated La Villemarqué in a decisive manner on one essential point. Donatien Laurent is an ethnologist, an eminent specialist on Breton civilization and folklore. In collecting popular Breton songs, he noticed he was gathering pieces that appeared in *Barzaz-Breiz*, but in forms that could not have been derived from it. That was an indication that these songs were not La Villemarqué's invention but that they truly existed independently of his book. Donatien Laurent pursued his research. For the first time, the La Villemarqué family opened the archives of their ancestor to him, and he was able to observe that *Barzaz-Breiz* was in fact based on a collection, whose starting point, as La Villemarqué had always said, was songs collected by his mother, "the lady of Nizon" (Marie-Ursule de Plessix-Nizon, countess de La Villemarqué), to whom the book is dedicated. Donatien Laurent's thesis thus rehabilitated La Villemarqué by demonstrating the reality of his field research, as Bernadette Bricout would do a few years later for Henri Pourrat and his tales.[35]

Why, under such conditions, and if La Villemarqué's cause was just, did he defend himself so little and so poorly? I shall pass over the details of the demonstration, but here in a word is Donatien Laurent's hypothesis, which is plausible and, for us, very enlightening. La Villemarqué did not publish what he had collected in its raw state, far from it. In accordance with a practice of the time—or rather, a practice that was already beginning to go out of fashion—he believed he was authorized to rearrange, rework, and at times rewrite the songs, with the help of local scholars, as a function of his taste and his aesthetic principles, as Arnim and Brentano, along with so many others, had done. Later, when philological method had progressed, his hand in it was detected, and he was called a counterfeiter. But by then, sensitive to the new requirements of scholarly publications, La Villemarqué, an elegant and scrupulous man ill suited for polemics, may have judged in his conscience that he had in fact been wrong to intervene so heavy-handedly in the texts and gave up the idea of producing the collection, which could have exonerated him of the most serious criticism, since it would have also confirmed his intervention.

But I wish to consider *Barzaz-Breiz* because it presupposes, in a particularly explicit and insistent manner, a link and a continuity between the Middle Ages and the Breton songs La Villemarqué and his mother may have heard, a link established through historical memories of which these Breton songs preserve the trace. His introduction is full of bards and druids; the author believes he can detect their activity until the late Middle Ages and their memory even in songs still alive during his own time. In his introduction and in the notes that accompany the pieces in the collection, he makes the greatest effort to link them to historical events or individuals, to establish that they are contemporary to these events, however remote they might be. A ridiculous demonstration, of course, and yet rather touching. But what especially interests us here are the songs that stand in relation to medieval literature: those that represent Arthur (*Arthur's March*; *Saint Efflamm and King Arthur*) or Merlin (*Merlin, Fragments of Ballads. 1. Merlin in the Cradle. 2. Merlin the Diviner. 3. Merlin the Bard. 4. Merlin's Conversion*), or, within the confines of history and literature, *Heloise and Abelard*, a beautiful poem in Heloise's voice, which makes her a student of Abelard/Merlin à la Anaïs Nin. In addition, two songs are the exact copies of medieval poems. The first is *Le rossignol* (The nightingale), which is Marie de France's lai *Laüstic*. As for the second, it consists of two episodes from *Les-Breiz*, "epic fragments," and, according to La Villemarqué, devoted to Murman (he calls him Morvan), the Breton king defeated and killed in combat against Louis the Pious in September 818, as related by Ermoldus Nigelus at the beginning of book 3 of his poem.[36] In the first of these episodes ("The Departure") we find the encounter between Perceval and the knights from the beginning of Chrétien de Troyes's *Conte du*

Graal; in the second ("The Return"), Perceval's return to his mother's castle and the reunion with his sister from the *Second Continuation of Perceval*.[37]

La Villemarqué himself calls attention to the truly stunning similarities. What are we to think of them? Neither *Le rossignol* nor *Lez-Breiz* appears among the songs collected by Donatien Laurent in our own time. These are cases in which one might without injustice suspect the author of *Barzaz-Breiz* of having added something of his own invention. Nonetheless, I do not believe he invented these poems from whole cloth, since then the commentaries he made on them and the relation he supposes between them and medieval texts would attest to a kind of impudence and provocation which was hardly in his character. The most plausible conjecture is that he was struck by an analogy between the popular Breton songs that really existed and the medieval poems that his attendance at the courses of the Ecole des Chartes had revealed to him. In his own way, lying in good faith as they say (though that is unkind to poor La Villemarqué), he had to force the resemblance somewhat. But if that is the case, his poems are only the more significant of the idea he had of popular poetry and of its situation with respect to medieval poetry.

In both cases, he assumes that the Breton songs predate the medieval poems. The art of the trouvères would accordingly have flourished—meagerly, to believe him, and with wilted flowers—beginning with the popular songs. These popular songs then supposedly survived the art of the trouvères and became inscribed in the very long term (from the beginnings of the Common Era, if not before, until the middle of the nineteenth century!). Marie de France herself provides him with an argument when she asserts that her lais are derived from Breton lais. *Le rossignol* as one reads it in *Barzaz-Breiz* would be nothing less than the model for the lai *Laüstic*:

> Since this ballad was known to Marie de France, and already popular at the time when this charming trouvère, who imitated it, was alive, we do not hesitate to believe it prior to the thirteenth century. We heard it sung in Cornouaille, in the mountains of Arez; but it must have been composed in Léon, since it belongs more

particularly to the dialect of that region. The event that is its subject has little importance in itself. The Breton singer does no more than indicate it, Marie de France spins it out.[38]

Does she spin it out? It is true that the song in *Barzaz-Breiz* is shorter (70 lines divided into distiches, or couplets, of octosyllables) than Marie de France's lai (160 lines in couplets of octosyllables) and that it is very allusive. Conversely, from the account of the initial situation to the description of the reliquary where the young man has the bird's body laid out, the lai relates the events in the order in which they occurred without omitting anything. Without omitting anything? Of course, Marie de France gravely relates everything that happened. But she maintains a deafening silence on the essential matter: the obvious and mysterious link between the nightingale and love. Getting up at night to listen to the nightingale is much more than an artifice that allows the lovers to see each other. It is the life of love, it is love itself. The murder of the nightingale, the little body spitefully thrown onto the lady's chemise by the jealous husband, the bloodied chemise, all signify an attack on love itself. Marie de France does not say so, she who feigns to say everything. She is so discreet that she veils the ellipsis from which her narrative draws its charm and its sense.

That is what La Villemarqué does not seem to see. He is only sensitive to the fact that the Breton song applies the aesthetic principles of the ballad, as the *Stürmer und Dränger* formulated them, for example, and that it manifests the characteristics attributed to popular songs: the beginning *in media res*, the importance of dialogue, ternary repetition and variations, breaks and inconsistencies in the narration, allusions and ellipses. It opens with the lament of the young woman, grieving for the death of the nightingale, and continues with the dialogue (which took place earlier) between her and her husband, who is curious to know why she gets up at night:

The young wife of Saint-Malo was crying yesterday at her high window;
"Alas! Alas! All is lost! My poor nightingale is killed!"

"Tell me, my new wife, why do you get up so often,
So often from beside me, in the middle of the night, from my bed?"[39]

The young woman declares it is to see the great ships, then that it is to look at her infant in its cradle, before confessing it is to hear the nightingale. It is only in the last lines, once the husband has had the bird killed and has thrown it "onto the white bosom of the lady," that "the young servant of love," of whom there has been no mention until now, intervenes to conclude the poem:

> Learning the news, the young servant of love said very sadly:
> "Now we are caught, my sweetheart and I; we will not be able
> to see each other again,
> By the moonlight, at the window, as was our habit."[40]

The sense of the little drama thus becomes clear retrospectively, and the young man's lament at the end of the song corresponds to that of the young woman, which, in a kind of anticipation of the narrative, constitutes its first words. The words of the "young servant of love" correspond almost exactly to those that Marie de France attributes to the lady:

> "Lasse," fet ele, "mal m'estait!
> Ne purrai mes la nuit lever
> N'aler a la fenestre ester
> U jeo sueil mun ami veeir."

> "Alas," she said, "now I must suffer!
> I won't be able to get up at night
> or go and stand in the window
> where I used to see my love."[41]

That resemblance is no doubt not fortuitous. Even though it is reckless to express an opinion without being able to judge from the Breton text, I seem to sense La Villemarqué's intervention: The "as was our habit" (*selon notre habitude*), a rather awkward translation, evokes the familiar little problem (elegantly resolved by Laurence Harf-Lancner) raised by the translation of the brief and rapid *sueil* from Old French.[42] But the author of *Barzaz-Breiz* believed in all good faith that the piece he was publishing, laden with "popular" traits, predated Marie de France's lai, from which these traits are absent, and was its source. That is hardly a credible hypothesis, but it shows that in his view the characteristics of popular poetry were quite naturally synonymous with antiquity. A song that forcefully displays these characteristics would be by rights older than a medieval work from which they are absent.

In addition, when we ourselves attempt to imagine the Breton lais—about which we know nothing—that served as models for Marie de France's narrative lais, we easily imagine them as musical compositions whose words would have made only incomplete, haplological allusions to the adventure that the Anglo-Norman poetess then reconstituted and recounted in its integrity. What we imagine is not very far from *Le rossignol* in *Barzaz-Breiz*. That does not mean, however, that La Villemarqué was right; it only means that perhaps even today we continue to be wrong with him.

There is a similar relationship between *Les-Breiz* and the medieval texts close to it, except that Chrétien de Troyes and his continuators never claimed to be inspired by Breton lais. The encounter between "the child Lez-Breiz" and the knight, his departure from his mother's manor, are, as it were, a summary of the beginning of the *Conte du Graal*, with a few almost verbatim quotations. For example, the remark inspired in Les-Breiz by the knight's armor—"If hinds were harnessed like that, it would be more difficult to kill them"[43]—is identical to Perceval's:

> —Danz chevalier, de tes hauberz
> Guart Dex les biches et les cerz,
> Que nus ocirre n'en porroie.

> "Oh, sir knight, may God keep all the hinds
> and stags from such hauberks,
> or I'd never kill one."[44]

Or again, there is the naive question that immediately follows— "But tell me, lord, were you born like that?"—which is the same as that posed by Perceval: "Fustes vos ensin nez?" (line 276). It draws the same response, the designation of the person who makes knights, the count of Quimper in one case, King Arthur in the other.

Elsewhere, the quotation is out of place. Les-Breiz declares to his mother that the knight he saw was "a more beautiful man than Sir Michael the archangel, who is in our church." To which the mother replies: "Yet there is no man more beautiful, more beautiful, my son, than the angels of our god." That echoes the reflection Perceval makes to himself at the arrival of the knights:

> Biaus sire Dex, merci!
> Ce sont ange que je voi ci . . .
> Ne me dist pas ma mere fable
> Qui me dist que li ange sont
> Les plus beles choses qui sont
> Fors Deu qui est est plus bel que tuit. .
> Si voi je Damedeu, ce cuit,
> Car un si bel en i esgart
> Que li autre, se Dex me gart,
> N'ont mie de biauté lo disme.

> Oh, thank you, God!
> These are angels I see here! . . .
> My mother told me no fable
> when she said that angels
> were the fairest things there are,
> except God, whose beauty surpasses all other.
> But there, I think,
> I see God Himself!
> For I can see one so fair
> that, God defend me,
> The others are not one tenth as beautiful.[45]

And soon, prostrated before the knight, he asks:

> —Estes vos Dex?—Nenil, par foi.
> —Qui estes vos?—Chevaliers sui.
> —Ainz mes chevalier ne conui,
> Fait le vallez, ne nul n'en vi

N'onques mes parler n'en oï,
Mais vos estes plus bes que Dex.

"Are you God?" "No, in faith!"
"Who are you, then?" "I am a knight."
"I have never met a knight before,"
the boy said, "or even seen
or heard of them;
but you are more beautiful than God."[46]

In this case, however, the difference is significant. The short passage from *Barzaz-Breiz* simply means to show the naivete of a popular piety that feeds on an admiration of images seen in churches—something not unrelated to the devotion François Villon attributes to his mother in *La ballade pour prier Notre Dame* (His Mother's Service to Our Lady):

Femme je suis, povrecte et ancïenne,
Qui riens ne sçay: oncques lettres ne leuz.
Au moustier voy, dont suis paroissienne,
Paradiz paint, où sont harpes et leuz,
Et ung enffer où dampnes sont bouluz.
L'un me fait paour, l'autre joye et lïesse.

A pitiful poor woman, shrunk and old,
I am, and nothing learn'd in letter-lore
Within my parish-cloister I behold
A painted Heaven where harps and lutes adore
And eke an Hell whose damned folk seethe full sore
One bringeth fear, the other joy to me.[47]

The archangel is figured as a man, seen as a man, as the most beautiful of men, more beautiful than the angels. Simple folk, the poem suggests, need images, concrete representations, and they imagine spiritual realities and creatures based on them. That is also what Perceval does. But not content to take for angels these men in shining armor (and that is, in fact, how Saint Michael is depicted), he takes the most beautiful of them to be God himself, on the pretext that God is more beautiful than the angels. He confuses the creature and the Creator. Similarly, he is satisfied with the appearance of the knight (his armor), not understanding that it is only the sign of the skill and moral qualities that alone make the knight. He also has no idea of progress, of apprenticeship, of education. He believes the knight was born in his armor, that everything is innate, that everything comes from nature. In Chrétien, all the formulations, all the details of the scene are thus adjusted with precision and humor to fit the vigorous thought and elevated spirituality of which they are the expression.

But these positive qualities are hardly considered such by La Ville-marqué, who seeks and relishes only naive simplicity, the guarantee in his view both of antiquity and of popular character. In *Le conte du Graal*, the character is naive, but the author hardly is. La Villemarqué deduces from this that *Les-Breiz* is the older poem (does it not celebrate an adversary of Louis the Pious?). It was supposedly imitated by the Welsh *Peredur*, which was then imitated by Chrétien de Troyes and Wolfram von Eschenbach.[48] In addition, he compares the encounter with the knight and the hero's departure not with the French romance but with the *mabinogi*. And, having cited the passage from the *Second Continuation of Perceval* (attributing it to Chrétien), which corresponds to the return of Les-Breiz, La Villemarqué comments:

> One obviously senses paraphrase and imitation here, as an excellent judge has noted (M. C. Magnin, *Journal des Savants*, 1847, p. 455). The French trouvère has no better luck than the Welsh storyteller; like him, he makes only a cold copy of an original and charming model. . . . It is not, in fact, the only time that the trouvères spoiled rustic traditions in putting a hand to them; we shall see other examples. It is as if some national memories are like those delicate plants that can only live and bloom in the places where they originated.[49]

La Villemarqué's harshness toward the medieval poem is not totally without foundation in this case. He judges the luxury in which Perceval's sister lives out of place, since she ought to be a poverty-stricken orphan in the recesses of a *gaste* castle—a ruined castle. The author of the *Second Continuation* seems to have composed his scene based on elements from two episodes of *Le conte du Graal*: Perceval's reception by the Rich Fisherman, from which he borrows the luxury of the castle and the meal, and the encounter between Perceval and his cousin, which gives him the model for the question: "Where did you spend the night?" But that is proof that the tale is not inspired by "rustic traditions"! Moreover, its awkwardness, if there is awkwardness, is laden with meaning: To write that crucial scene, the author draws from passages that, in the work of his predecessor, lie at the heart of the family mystery.

La Villemarqué does not indulge in that sort of consideration. He simply judges the quality of medieval literature by the yardstick of popular poetry and by the same criteria—and as a result, he judges it harshly. He sees that it is not popular, but only to deplore the fact that it has strayed from the vein he judges necessarily the primary and only authentic one. According to him, the medieval trouvères exploited and deformed "rustic traditions," which have survived in folklore until the modern era. These traditions are in his view rooted in history, and they preserve "national memories." Allusive and fragmentary (think of the title *Lez-Breiz: Epic fragments*), popular Breton songs by their characteristics manifest an anteriority in relation to medieval poems, which seek coherence, which "spin out," which gain in refinement and lose in sensitivity. Laugh if you like, and it is quite true that the filiation of Les-Breiz and Chrétien de Troyes via *Peredur* can make us smile. But when we compare the anonymous *chansons de toile* with those of Audefroi le Bâtard, is it not the same criteria that make us judge the former much older than the latter? The acknowledgment of the nonpopular character of medieval literature goes hand in hand with the effort to follow the traces of a popular literature back to the Middle Ages.

Thus we are led back to the questions raised by the Fortoul survey with which we began. La Villemarqué, in his introduction to the 1867 edition of *Barzaz-Breiz*, mentions it and a similar survey launched during the July monarchy by a predecessor of Fortoul, count de Salvandy, whose strongly ideological program he cites with emotion:

> To bring together poems devoted to religion, to its memory, to its precepts, which the people sing in each of the provinces of France; all those that concern brilliant events of national history; all the

traditional songs of a nature to teach the people of the cities and countryside to love God, their nation, and their duties.[50]

Thus we are led back to the Fortoul survey, because, in Ampère's instructions, it crystallizes and summarizes the debate of those years—roughly, the 1840s: Fauriel had been teaching at the Sorbonne since 1830; O. L. B. Wolff's *Altfranzösische Lieder* appeared in 1831; Francisque Michel, sent to Oxford in 1833 by Guizot, minister of public education at the time, discovered the manuscript of *La chanson de Roland* there in 1835; *Barzaz-Breiz* dates from 1839; Le Roux de Lincy's *Recueil de chants historiques français depuis le XIIe jusqu'au XIVe siècle* dates from 1841; Uhland published his *Alte hoch- und niederdeutsche Volkslieder* in 1844 and 1845; the Salvandy survey was launched in 1845; Wackernagel published his *Altfranzoesische Lieder und Leiche* in 1846 and Diez his *Altromanische Sprachdenkmale* the same year; and Prosper Tarbé produced many hasty editions of poetry by the trouvères and of chansons de geste beginning in 1849. At the beginning of the 1850s, it was acknowledged that the poetry of the Middle Ages was not a popular poetry, but no one gave up the conviction that the first manifestations of poetry were popular, that the essence of popular poetry was in the past, and that collecting popular poems was a means for moving back in time. How, from their point of view, and particularly in the field of lyric poetry and song, were medievalists going to get out of that increasingly tangled web?

From the establishment of Romance philology as a rigorous science in the middle of the last century until today, distinguishing between what is popular and what is not has truly been a constant preoccupation of medievalists; it is sometimes explicit, sometimes latent, and it can be felt at every moment in the interminable debate devoted to the origins of Romance literatures. That debate has dealt almost exclusively with song, since its two privileged objects are the chansons de geste and lyric poetry. And the concern to distinguish what is popular from what is not brought about a quest for origins, because the tendency of scholars has always been to cast the popular back into a past prior to the extant texts.

The Temptation of
a Prehistory

On Medievalists, Women, and Song

The oldest medieval poetry we know of was new in its time. It was not popular but aristocratic. These points were established even before the middle of the nineteenth century. Nonetheless, medievalists did not despair of reaching a more ancient stratum of popular poetry through that medieval poetry, a stratum it might conceal. Despite the break achieved between the poetry of the Middle Ages and popular songs, those who studied both fields long remained anxious to reach the underlying stratum.

Students of popular song were anxious for several reasons. In the first place, it is difficult to be interested in popular song without giving it credit a priori for a spontaneity, a natural character, which would be proof of its antiquity and the mark of an authenticity and a superiority over other forms of poetry. We have seen that Montaigne's remarks already implied as much. This is particularly true when one takes into account a reflection on music, as the study of song requires. Music, easily considered an expression of human affectivity more spontaneous than poetry, because the intellect plays less of a role in it than it does in language, seeks its roots in its most simple manifestations. Even more than poets in their order, musicians like to exploit traditional and popular timbres. In 1785, during the time of both the troubadour style and Rousseauism, Chabanon wrote: "The first step that [French music] took away from simple and popular songs (like those of the old carols) turned it away from its true path."[1] As we continue to move back and forth between the past of history and the personal past, how can we not link these lines to what Pascal Quignard has recently written—using the image of the raw and the cooked, which does not lead us far from Lévi-Strauss: "Nothing raw in language. Language too close to cooking. All that is said is cooked. Language always come too late upon us. Prehistory, archaism of music in us."[2]

A century after Chabanon, in 1889, Julien Tiersot concluded his *Histoire de la chanson populaire en France* (History of popular song in France) with the wish that modern music might reestablish its ties with "the spontaneity of the lyricism of our ancestors," and he applied the old romantic idea of ethnic identity and genius conserved and revealed by art to his vision of the future: "And perhaps, from that union of modern science with the spontaneity of the lyricism of our ancestors, there will emerge one day one of those significant works that marks a date and deserves to endure because it reveals, in clear and brilliant fashion, the age-old tastes and eternal genius of a race."[3]

In addition, specialists in popular song, less informed about the reality of medieval literature or less prudent than those who devote themselves to its study, have been less hesitant to trace it back continuously to the earliest Middle Ages and to note pell-mell, without taking too many precautions, several pieces of evidence that are always invoked on the subject: from Césaire d'Arles; from the Council of Châlons in 650; from Hildegaire's cantilena of Saint Faron; from William of Malmesbury; and from Wace on the jongleur Taillefer at the Battle of Hastings. Weckerlin cites them in 1887, M. Tresch in 1921.[4]

In a more rigorous and more solid way, metrists have posited a certain continuity between medieval lyricism and popular song. Whatever Nerval's errors of detail, he was right to see in meter, in rhythm, and in the hesitation between assonance and rhyme the historical and aesthetic key to popular song. That vein was productively tapped by Paul Verrier and is today being tapped by Conrad Laforte. Verrier saw the "carol distich" followed by refrain, a form designed to accompany dance, as the metric foundation of Romance lyricism.[5] Laforte links the medieval laisse to the long homophonic lines with strong caesura characteristic of the French popular song.[6]

Among medievalists, the same effort was made to point out the traces of a popular poetry before that of the troubadours and the trouvères, but that effort soon changed direction because of Joseph Bédier's conceptions and those of his disciples—"individualism," as it is called—and then because of the new conditions created by the opposition between that individualism and a current associated with Ramón Menéndez Pidal, which defined itself as "neotraditionalist."

In that reflection and in that research, one work played an important role from the beginning, Karl Bartsch's *Altfranzösische Romanzen und Pastourellen* (Romances and pastourelles in Old French), published in Leipzig in 1870. This is a critical edition of twelfth- and thirteenth-century poems published in langue d'oïl; it consists of all such poems known to the author which escaped courtly inspiration and could be linked to a popular or popularistic vein. Under the name "romances," that old term whose fortunes we briefly noted, Bartsch first placed the *chansons de toile*. They may deserve that designation because of their narrative character, their form similar to the chanson de geste, their stiffness, and their simplicity. Bartsch added a disparate series of women's songs, narrative songs, aubades, dancing songs, and songs of amorous encounters, whose only common trait is that the spirit of *fin'amor* is absent from them. As for the pastourelles, these are, as we know, narrative and dramatic songs in which the narrator tells how, and with what success, he attempted to seduce a shepherdess, or in which he describes shepherds' exploits. These pieces, as was observed well before Bartsch, are not in the least popular, but they cast their gaze on the rustic world and its loves.

This heteroclite set was so well and so quickly erected into a canonical corpus that when, twenty-five years later, Alfred Jeanroy wrote his thesis *Les origines de la poésie lyrique en France au Moyen*

Age, he devoted the first chapter to the pastourelles, and the first words of this chapter to the work of Bartsch. By his own admission, Bartsch's work defined the pastourelles:

> We must admit: great is the reader's disappointment in perusing for the first time the volume published by Bartsch, or at least the last two parts of this volume [i.e., those devoted to the pastourelles], which make up nearly the whole of it. The editor has just noted that it brings together "the most important and most characteristic forms of the lyric from the north of France, next to which all the others pale in comparison" (*Einleit.*, p. v): we thus expect to see unfolding before our eyes, in their infinite diversity, the naive and poetic conceptions of the spirit of the people or the original fancies of their imagination; we expect to encounter along our route tableaux that are bold perhaps, or strange, but simple and varied. These expectations are, in short, singularly disappointed.[7]

Even though he claims to be disappointed—and curiously, that will be his constant feeling about this poetry to which he devoted his life—and even though one might understand it under the circumstances, since the bawdy monotony of the pastourelles are disconcerting enough at first encounter, Jeanroy admits that Bartsch collected the songs that were closest to what could have been a popular lyricism in the Middle Ages. And what does Bartsch himself think of that? His short introduction opens with these words:

> If I have brought together romances and pastourelles in Old French, it is not by chance but for good reason. Both have popular foundations and both appropriated popular elements. Given the regrettable loss that has afflicted popular lyricism in Romance language of the Middle Ages, they are thus of great value; they constitute the most important genres of the lyric from the north of France, next to which all the others pale in comparison, and are eclipsed by the richer ones from the south of France.[8]

To say that romances and pastourelles have a popular foundation and contain popular elements is to imply they are not themselves popular songs. They only give an idea, but a precious idea, of what Romance popular lyric—unfortunately lost because covered over by the courtly poetry of the troubadours—might have been. The end of the paragraph, cited in part by Jeanroy, means simply that the courtly poetry of the trouvères adds nothing very remarkable to that of the troubadours and that the true originality of the lyricism in langue d'oïl is to have conserved these traces of popular poetry. That is the very proposition that Jeanroy's thesis sets itself the task of examining.[9]

We will not take up that examination here. We will not summarize in a few minutes or in an hour a scholarly debate that has lasted for a century and that has been partially renewed since the last war by the discovery, or rather the decipherment, of the Mozarabic *khardjas*. It is a debate in which I have already taken some superficial interest and of which recent summaries exist.[10] We will confine ourselves to illustrating once more, based on the items in this dossier, the idea we have harped on since the beginning. Scholars recognized very early on that these "noncourtly" songs were not in themselves truly popular but displayed popular characteristics that stood in contrast to a learned lyricism (*canso* or *muwwashah*). Based on our knowledge of medieval poetry, that learned lyricism was preexistent. Some scholars nonetheless supposed that these songs derived from a more ancient tradition that was authentically popular and had been lost. Others, in reaction to that hypothesis, maintained that arguments ought to be based only on extant texts and that it was possible to account for these songs as imitations of Latin models. Or they put forward the traits borrowed from courtly lyricism and argued that these poems were solely an excrescence of that lyricism. That is Faral's and Delbouille's position on the pastourelles—though they insist excessively on the so-called imitation of Latin models—and it is also Faral's position, in a much more subtle and convincing way, on the *chansons de toile*.[11] Like them, I would like to relate these supposedly popular pieces to the learned lyricism from within which they emerged, but only to advance the idea that the popular character of such songs was defined on the basis of that contrast, which itself gives credence to the suggestion of an old tradition. The poetry of the *chansons de toile* was thus perceived in the thirteenth century as the songs of the Valois were perceived in the nineteenth.

I do not have the leisure to pursue that demonstration very far. But I shall indicate the key points: One is the fact that these are women's songs; the other is their versification. If I had the competence necessary, I would also speak of the melodies.

Women's songs: That fact is immediately striking. Courtly lyricism rests on a representation of male desire. It is nothing but the vertigo of frustration, a fevered and daring imagination frightened by the female body and by an impossible satisfaction, the expectation of a hoped-for gift. Never does the lover imagine that the lady's desire might mirror his own; never does he seek to awaken it. He expects the lady to reward faithful love, not to give in to the call of the flesh. She is, as Bernard de Ventadour imagines her, like snow: immaculate and frigid, and it is only her extreme coldness that gives the illusion of burning. In a word, *fin'amor*—and this may be its true originality—refuses to see woman as the creature the Fathers of the Church and the moralists warn against, a creature subjected to the demands of the body and to its appetites, because her intelligence and her will are too weak to dominate them.

In contrast, the noncourtly side of lyric poetry construes love as a woman's feeling and, in accordance with a more traditional vision, subjects woman to desire, has her express it with a lewd and grave simplicity. How are we to doubt that this type of poetry is ancient? These are the indecent women's songs that the Council of Châlons condemned in 650. This is the female voice resonating in the *khardjas*. This is the voice we hear, going back even further and leaving the Romance field, in classical literature, from Andromaque to Penelope, from Deianira to Medea to Dido, and all around the Mediterranean basin, as Elvira Gangutia Elicegui has shown.[12] On Cyprus, the sacred prostitute sitting at her window has the same attitude as the young lady in the *chansons de toile*—and later as Saint Agnes. The first *Minnesänger* affected a female voice, as did the knight of Kürenberg about 1150, before their poetry drew inspiration from the Occitan and French model; and even then, Walther von der Vogelweide composed *Unter der Linde*, and Marcabru composed *A la fontana del vergier*. In langue d'oïl, the female voice is that of certain crusade songs, like Guiot de Dijon's notorious *Chanterai por mon corage* or *Jherusalem, grant damage me fais*, that of the *chansons de toile*; and that of the lovely Aude, contrasting with Roland's indifference in his last hour. It is also, in the chanson de geste *Ami et Amile*, the voice of Bélissant, daughter of Charlemagne, who insists on sleeping with a timorous Amile.[13] It is, even more markedly, the voice of the Gallician Portuguese *cantigas d'amigo*. It is almost always a disguised male voice. At the end of the *chanson de toile Oriolanz en haut solier* (Oriolant in a high chamber), the poet reveals himself:

> Et je, qui ceste chanson fis,
> Sor la rive de mer pansis,
> Comanz a Deu bele Aelis.[14]

> And I, who made this song,
> On the seashore, pensive,
> I recommend the lovely Aélis to God.

It is as if a particular form of sensuality could find expression only when ascribed, albeit fictively, to women. A form of sensuality that is sometimes fleetingly heard even in the *trobairitz*, ordinarily so dependent on the male model of poetry and love. Finally, in the French songs of the fifteenth century, the female voice easily appropriates for itself the theme of the trouvères: From then on, the pastourelles are presented from the point of view of the shepherdess. As a result, she becomes virtuous. Many later popular songs echo this: *Derrière chez nous, il y a un étang / Trois beaux canards y vont nageant* (Behind our house there is a pond / Three lovely ducks go swimming there), particularly in the versions in which the refrain implicitly rejects a proposition from a prince—"Mais moi je préfère un petit moulin sur la rivière / Et puis encore un petit bateau pour passer l'eau" (But I prefer a little mill on the river / And even more a little boat to cross the water)—and *Mon père avait cinq cents moutons* (My father had five hundred sheep). That is also the case for an ancestor of that last song, a song from the fifteenth century of which we shall speak again. Its narrator is the knight in the first two stanzas, but the narrative then shifts to the third person and the seducer is dispatched.[15]

How, under these conditions, could we not imagine a tradition lost in the mists of time but which has endured to our own era in folklore? Efforts in that direction were made by Alfred Jeanroy, who also took on the rather pointless task of showing the anteriority of French lyric poetry in relation to that of the rest of Europe, and Gaston Paris, who defended and illustrated the ideas of his student, Joseph Bédier himself, with the theory of the May Day celebrations, though Bédier was by nature little inclined toward that type of hypothesis.[16] In their view, the first Romance lyricism accompanied celebrations of spring renewal, certain manifestations of which have been preserved almost to our own time: hence the systematic presence of a "springtime stanza" at the beginning of songs by the troubadours and trouvères. These celebrations were supposedly marked by a certain license and a reversal of the usual roles, with the result that the initiative in love was left to the women: hence the tradition of women's songs. Some believed they had found a direct echo of these practices in certain songs, like the famous ballad of the queen of April *A l'entrada des temps clar, Eya* (With the entrance of clear weather, Eya).[17] Gaston Paris wanted to place the birthplace of that lyricism within the boundaries of Poitou and Limousin, a linguistic border country that would explain the mixture of langue d'oc and langue d'oïl, or langue d'oïl with a flavor of langue d'oc, in the *Ballade de la reine d'avril* and a few other pieces, such as the charming song of spring *Volés vos que je vous chant / Un son d'amor avenant* (Would you like me to sing / An appealing song of love).[18] In this song, the daughter of the nightingale and the siren is not only arrayed but actually dressed in the flowers of spring (shoes of gladiolus) with a girdle of foliage that becomes greener when the weather is damp, while on the croup of her mule three rose bushes are planted "to provide her with shade."

It has been quite easy since then to denounce the fragility of that framework, to show that the *Ballade de la reine d'avril* and the songs that might stem from a similar inspiration are not especially old, that the theme of the *malmariée* and of her jealous husband is closely linked to the courtly world, that the song of the daughter of the nightingale and the siren claims it was composed by a knight and not by a villein. The artifice of Occitan desinences tacked onto langue d'oïl hardly argues in favor of an ancient, popular, and in some way spontaneous poetry. On the contrary, it suggests an imitation of an already prestigious poetry in langue d'oc. But did the hypothesis require that one go back in time? Why see these songs at all cost as the vestiges of a state of lyricism prior to the troubadours? Why wish that the phenomena associated with May Day celebrations be necessarily lost in the mists of time, when these celebrations, though of course ancient in themselves, have continued to exist to the modern era? At the end of the twelfth century and during the thirteenth, songs referred to the joy of love during the renewal of spring, to the license permitted in that season to women's loves; they played on simplicity, referred with some ostentation to traditional practices and beliefs, but showed as well that they were not unaware of courtly inspiration and conventions. Why not take them for what they are? Songs whose simplicity and sensuality, marked by, among other things, their character as women's songs, do not exist in themselves and whose antiquity is not real. That character and that antiquity have meaning only in reference and intentional opposition to the conventions of love and poetry of the *grand chant courtois*. One might, if one wished, call that vein popularistic, but it is conscious of being so. In addition, and once more, the very notion of "the popular" can exist only in opposition to a learned poetry. The contrast between the elevated language of the seducer and the rustic language of the shepherdess, which gives the pastourelles their captivating quality,[19] opposes women's songs generally to other modes of lyric expression. The heroine of the *chansons de toile* is not coarse like the shepherdess. But she does not discourse on the nature of love and the nuances of feeling as a trouvère would do within the framework of a *grand chant courtois*. She knows only to say that she loves, and to offer herself to the one she loves, substituting for the discourse on love the gestures of love.[20] The stiffness of homophonic stanzas and paratactic sentences poured into the crude decasyllabic meter seems characteristic of her.

The versification that goes hand in hand with that inspiration also covers the entire gamut of simplicity: homophony of the laisses in the *chansons de toile*; homophony, marked by the simplistic cry of jubilation "Eya!" in the stanza *A l'entrada des temps clar*—with the exception of the final line and the refrain; elementary stanza structures in ababab(ab), derived from three or four long lines interrupted by internal rhyme,[21] such as that used by Guiot de Dijon in *Chanterai por mon corage*; tailed stanza, formed of two bracketed tercets, in *Volés vos que je vos chant*; fixed and simple form of the rondeau, which looks very much like the slight development of the distich in the carol. And everywhere there is the refrain, which is systematically absent from the *grand chant courtois*. Finally, there is the simplicity of repetitive melodies—at least until the final cadence—which follow the homophony of the stanza (in *A l'entrada des temps clar* and certain *chansons de toile—En un vergier lès une fontenelle, Belle Yolanz en ses chambres seoit*) or have only one variation, corresponding to the *b* rhyme, as in the rondeau. This is an intentional simplicity, since, conversely, certain *chansons de toile* have a very ornate melody, like *Belle Doette*, whose "modern" or mannered traits Faral demonstrated: The lovely Doette is not occupied with needlework but "reads in a book"; her sweetheart did not die in the war but in a tournament; she does not die of sorrow, like the lovely Aude, but wants to found a convent where faithful lovers can seek refuge.

Belle Aiglentine

This does not mean that these forms are not old, but simply that they were alive at the moment we catch sight of them only because opposing forms gave them meaning. In the *Roman de la rose ou de Guillaume de Dole*, the brilliant and frivolous life led at the emperor's court is contrasted to the remote and provincial life led by Liénor and her mother, outside time and beyond the world. This contrast lies at the foundation of the narrative, for it is a necessary element of the so-called wager tale.[22] Jean Renart takes care to express it in, among other ways, the choice of songs he is so proud to insert pertinently into his romance. Songs of love by Bernard de Ventadour, Jaufré Rudel, Gace Brulé, and many other poets in vogue are sung at court. Liénor and her mother, embarrassed by their antiquated repertoire, timidly sing *chansons de toile* while working on their pious embroidery; these songs depict a mother and her daughter—the latter sweetly but obstinately in love—occupied at the same task. That is all very well known, and I myself had the occasion to propose a commentary on these songs a long time ago.[23] But in Jean Renart's romance we find another *chanson de toile*, whose insertion into a completely different context seems to belie that contrast but in reality confirms and enriches it. That is the song *Belle Aiglentine*. Here it is as it appears in the manuscript:

> I. Bele Aiglentine en roial chamberine
> Devant sa dame cousoit une chemise.
> Ainc n'en sot rien quant bone amor l'atise.
> Or orrez ja
> Conment la bele Aiglentine esploita.
>
> II. Devant sa dame cousoit et si tailloit.
> Mes ne coust mie si com coudre soloit:
> El s'entroublie, si se point en son doit.
> La soe mere mout tost s'en aperçoit.
> Or orrez ja
> Conment [la bele Aiglentine esploita.]
>
> III. —Bele Aiglentine, deffublez vo surcot:
> Je voil veoir desoz vostre gent cors.
> —Non ferai, dame, la froidure est la morz.
> Or orrez ja
> [Conment la bele Aiglentine esploita.]
>
> IV. —Bele Aiglentine, q'avez a empirier,
> Que si vos voi pallir et engroissier?
> —Ma douce dame, ne le vos puis noier:
> Je ai amé .I. cortois sodoier,
> Le preu Henri, qui tant fet a poisier.

S'onques m'amastes, aiez de moi pitié.
Or orrez ja
Conment [la bele Aiglentine esploita.]

V. —Bele Aiglentine, vos prendra il Henris?
—Ne sai voir, dame, car onques ne li quis.
—Bele Aiglentine, or vos tornez de ci.
Tot ce dites que ge li mant Henri
S'il vos prendra ou vos lera ensi.
—Volentiers, dame, la bele respondi.
Or orrez ja
[Conment la bele Aiglentine esploita.]

VI. Bele Aiglentine s'est tornee de ci,
Et est venue droit a l'ostel Henri.
Le quens Henris se gisoit en son lit.
Or orrez ja que la bele li dit
Or orrez ja
[Conment la bele Aiglentine esploita.]

VII. —Sire Henri, veilliez vos ou dormez?
Ja vos requiert Aiglen[tine] au vis cler
Se la prendrez a moullier et a per.
—Oïl, dil il, onc joie n'oi mes tel.
Or orrez ja
[Conment la bele Aiglentine esploita.]

VIII. Oit le Henris, mult joianz en devint.
Il fet monter chevaliers trusq'a.XX.,
Si enporta la bele en son païs
Et espousa: riche contesse en fist
Grant joie en a
Le quens Henris quant bele Aiglentine a.

In a royal chamber, beautiful Eglantine
Was sewing a shirt, with her mother there to see,
When thoughts of love enflamed her suddenly,
Now hear the tale—
Eglantine's wit did not fail.

She cuts and sews the cloth; the lady stays
Eglantine had more skill on other days.

She pricks her finger when her attention strays—
All this her mother notices right away.
Now hear the tale—
Eglantine's wit did not fail.

"Eglantine," said her mother, "please undress.
I want to see your body's loveliness."
"No my lady, it's cold; I'll catch my death."
Now hear the tale—
Eglantine's wit did not fail.

"Beautiful Eglantine, what is the matter?
It seems to me you're pale and growing fatter."
"From you, my gentle lady, I can't hide
The truth: I fell in love with a valiant knight;
That is Henri, in whom his lord takes pride.
So may your love take pity on my plight."
Now hear the tale—
Eglantine's wit did not fail.

"Eglantine, will the noble Henri marry you?"
"I don't know, mother, I never asked him to."
"My lovely Eglantine, go right away
And tell Henri from me that he must say
Whether he'll be your husband or leave you this way."
And Eglantine replied, "I will obey."
Now hear the tale—
Eglantine's wit did not fail.

From her mother's house fair Eglantine sped;
To Henri's lodging her footsteps led.
She found her lover lying in bed,
And you shall hear what words she said.
Now hear the tale—
Eglantine's wit did not fail.

"Are you awake or sleeping, my lord knight?
Eglantine, whose eyes like stars are bright,
Asks if you'll have her for your wedded wife."
"Yes," said Henri, "I've not known such joy in my life."
Now hear the tale—
Eglantine's wit did not fail.

> Henri has listened to her with great delight.
> He quickly summons twenty of his knights
> And to his country joyfully they ride;
> Now she is his countess and his bride.
> How happy Count Henri is
> That the beautiful Eglantine is his![24]

The song is sung by a young man ("uns bachelers de Normendie," line 2231) at the festivities preceding the tournament of Saint-Trond; Jouglet, the emperor's jongleur, accompanies him on the hurdy-gurdy. It livens up an evening among men. That is understandable. It is a woman's song that is not meant for maidens. That story of a knocked-up girl who asks her sweetheart to make it legal would in fact be out of place if sung by Liénor and her mother. Here, then, is a *chanson de toile* that does not at all play the same role in the romance as others like it. Far from offering a reflection of the circumstances in which it is sung and of the characters who sing it, it is in dissonance with both. It is obviously with a humorous, perhaps even a farcical, intention that the young men in their cups sing that sentimental and female romance, in which the naivete of the heroine might elicit a bawdy wink. Fifty or sixty years later, Adam de la Halle's *Jeu de la Feuillée* offers a confirmation of the fact that the *chansons de toile* could be sung in that spirit: The inebriated drinkers in the tavern, whom the innkeeper invites to "bawl out" at the end of a parody of a sermon, sing *Aye se siet en haute tour*, before fishing for and receiving burlesque compliments.[25]

Let us leave these observations hanging for a moment and move on to another point, which in appearance has nothing to do with them. In the only manuscript of *Guillaume de Dole*, the song *Belle Aiglentine*, otherwise unknown, is, as we may note, made up of stanzas of irregular length, with between two and four lines. Two efforts have been made to correct that irregularity. According to Félix Lecoy, the editor of the romance, all the stanzas ought to be of four lines. For those that are shorter, lines must have been omitted.[26] According to Paul Zumthor, who devotes a long analysis to the song, the stanzas were originally tercets. But in the only copy we possess, the third line of the tercet may sometimes have slipped to the beginning of the following stanza, in the interest of maintaining the same assonance in two consecutive stanzas—thus the poem ends with a two-line stanza followed by a four-line stanza—while elsewhere a fourth adventitious line may have been added to the tercet.[27] In the second case, the song would have been artificially lengthened by padding the narrative and by adding redundant lines: "La soe mere mout tost s'en aperçoit" (Her mother notices immediately); "Oïl, dit il, onc joie n'oi mes tel ("Yes," he said, "my joy has never been greater"); "Or orrez ja que la bele li dit" ("Listen then what the beauty said to him"). That last line, in fact, introduces an awkward repetition with the refrain that follows ("Or orrez ja / Conment la bele Aiglentine esploita"). If these lines are suppressed, everything speeds up: The mother and then Eglantine begin to speak without warning. Let us note that this use of ellipsis corresponds to the aesthetics traditionally attributed to popular song.

To suppose that the song was originally made up of tercets is thus once more to attribute implicitly a popular origin to it in a past prior to the time when we learn of it. Conversely, the text as we now know it would have been flattened and spun out (are we so far from the opinion of La Villemarqué about Marie de France?); at the same time, it would represent an evolution of literary art. In this instance, that evolution is confirmed by a precise association. We know that, in addition to about fifteen anonymous *chansons de toile*, we possess five that are the work of the trouvère Audefroi le Bâtard, whose literary activity took place in the first third of the thirteenth century. They are considered late imitations of an old genre. In reality, they are contemporary to the time when the anonymous songs, whose date of composition we do not know, were collected.[28] But it is true that, in relation to the anonymous songs, Audefroi le Bâtard's "prolix and insipid" songs (in G. Muraille's words) display traits analogous to those of the song *Belle Aiglentine* as we know it, compared with the hypothetical original version in tercets. In addition, one of Audefroi's songs, *En chambre a or se siet la belle Beatris*, which deals with the same theme, does so in a form that is much more developed but in which identical details, with additions, are also found. Hence, in the concluding stanza of *Belle Aiglentine*, Count Henry, leaving to marry his sweetheart, "fet monter chevalier trusq'a.XX." (had twenty knights mount on horseback). This line, which according to Paul Zumthor is one of the additions, reappears in *Belle Béatris*, but the number of knights is now fifty (lines 51–52).

It thus seems to us that these songs tend toward a kind of exhaustivity and narrative saturation, in contrast to the elliptical laconism we like to believe marks the genre in its beginnings. But that is not all. For on each occasion, Liénor and her mother sing only the first two stanzas of a song, which remains incomplete and lacunary. And, in a general way, with the exception of the dance rondeaux, which in any case have only one stanza but at the same time play on a perpetual suspense, Jean Renart never reproduces more than one or two stanzas of each song in *Guillaume de Dole*. *Belle Aiglentine* is the only one to be cited *in extenso*, and in fact, more than *in extenso*, if it is true the text has been lengthened.

The romance writer thus exploits a single image of the *chansons de toile* in two different ways. That image is of the obsolete, the outmoded, of awkward simplicity, and it is associated with the narrative women's song, which has homophonic stanzas similar to the epic laisse. Should he wish to depict a mother and her daughter, innocent and naive provincials living far from the world, secluded in an isolated castle, he makes them characters in a *chanson de toile* and has them sing *chansons de toile*. The mother and daughter, in the ladies' chamber, are occupied with pious embroidery and in turn sing *chansons de toile*, in which a mother and daughter, in the ladies' chamber, are occupied with pious embroidery. The mother's songs depict a severe mother, the daughter's songs a daughter in love. The supposed antiquity of the songs is underscored by the old woman ("Ladies and queens of days gone by were always singing spinning songs [*chançons d'istoire*, literally, "songs of history"—trans.] as they embroidered"), but is also suggested by the fragmentary quotations made of them.

Should Jean Renart then want to show the amusements of elegant youths, he again has them sing—among other things—a *chanson de toile*, but in a spirit of slight derision. That song—unrefined in the eyes of these lovers of courtly poetry—with its scabrous situation and its passive heroine, makes them smile. It is not limited to two stanzas drawn from a forgotten past, which would suffice to set the tone of the scene and mark its sensibility. It is sung from beginning to end, like the telling of a good story. And it is not only sung from beginning to end; it is added to perhaps, it is lengthened, making it even more clumsy, lengthened with adventitious lines that are so much narrative padding, if Paul Zumthor's hypothesis is valid. That amplification is even more prominent, but with identical elements, in Audefroi le Bâtard's *en chambre a or se siet la belle Beatris*. And that amplification corresponds to the tastes of the time.

Jean Renart thus uses the *chansons de toile*, sometimes to appear old-fashioned (and in that case, he cites them only in fragments and in such a way as to produce the effect of forgetting analyzed above), sometimes to get a laugh (and then, the piece is reproduced in its entirety). Both uses confirm the fact that the essential character of these songs is not to be in fashion. But we also see that to be sung in a fashionable milieu, even in a farcical manner, the text must no longer be given in fragmentary form but rather in its entirety, or even in more than its entirety, through a kind of oversaturation of the narrative. These songs, so happy to play with ellipsis even in their complete versions, as shown in the *chansonnier* of Saint-Germain-des-Prés, must be completed to the point of narrative exhaustivity. That is what Audefroi undertakes to do. That may also be what Jean Renart does, if we accept Paul Zumthor's view. But at the same time, the arrangement of the song on the page, with its concatenation of laisses of irregular length, increases the impression of awkwardness and archaism. The genius of Jean Renart—if he is responsible for that arrangement—is to have used the same trait (a form of amplification, the quest for narrative exhaustivity) to render the song somewhat to the taste of the day but also, and even though this appears contradictory, to increase the impression of its irregularity, of its unpolished clumsiness, of its awkward and outdated character. Similarly, as we saw above, he had the stroke of genius to associate truncated quota-

tions (which appear a few years later, but without particular signifi-
cance, in Gerbert de Montreuil and Henri d'Andeli)[29] with the designation "songs of history" for old songs now out of fashion and with
the antiquated and evanescent atmosphere of the entire scene.

In its mode of quotation, its context, and even its spirit, *Belle
Aiglentine* stands opposed to the other *chansons de toile*, those sung by
Liénor and her mother. Nevertheless, in its case as in theirs, the apparent devaluation and the real value of the song come explicitly
from the fact that it is presented as old. That is because the opposition between old song and new song is, as we shall now see, a fundamental element of medieval lyricism.

If Jean Renart had known Champfleury, he might have turned to
his own account, in reference to the *chansons de toile*, the mixture of
admiration and condescension which Champfleury showed toward
the popular song: "I like popular poetry with its clunky rhymes and
natural feeling."[30] Nearly a century later, under the Occupation,
Aragon sought popular and national inspiration from medieval poetry, which he knew very well, from *La leçon de Ribérac* to *Brocé-
liande*, in his *Diane française* and *Les yeux d'Elsa*. He combined simple rhymes inspired by popular or working-class songs ("Une
chanson vulgaire et douce où la voix baisse", A vulgar and sweet song
where the voice lowers) with the memory of Arnaut Daniel and
Bertrand de Born, the "so-called knight of the cart" or "Perceval in
his mother's garden." In a similar spirit no doubt, in the wake of the
Liberation Henry Poulaille and Régine Pernoud published the *chansons de toile*.[31] Régine Pernoud's introduction prudently underscores
the fact that they are at most "semipopular," that many scholars attribute "instead a literary character" to them, and that "for M.
Bédier, these songs are a learned creation." We may be allowed to
suppose, however, that in these very old songs, which are part of the
memory of a France whose resurrection was then being celebrated,
the populist novelist Henry Poulaille also loved "clunky rhymes and
natural feeling."

The Fresh Source of Songs

Old Song, New Song

The songs of the Middle Ages often claim to be new. Some, however, those that concern us here, present themselves as old. What novelty, what antiquity? What relation unites and opposes the two notions?

Before responding, let me make a final detour through the poetics of the refrain, a poetics that involves the irruption of antiquity within novelty. The refrain, systematically absent from the *grand chant courtois*, which claims to be new, and almost systematically present in the other lyric forms, is itself a reminiscence. But that reminiscence is not directly grounded in repetition. In the first place, the word *refrain*, from *refractum* ("broken," "torn away"), designates not an element that returns in identical form at the end of each stanza but an element that is cut off from the stanza, that does not truly belong to it, that is distinguished from it metrically or melodically or thematically, or all three at once. That is why numerous medieval refrains have been conserved in isolation but are nonetheless definable and recognizable as refrains.[1] That is why a type of song existed during the Middle Ages which was called, not "refrain song" (*à refrain*), but song "with refrains" (*avec des refrains*), in which each stanza ends in a different refrain. Thus, the refrain is not identifiable by its return within the song but is so formally, as an element isolated from the stanza by the meter and melody, and thematically, since it is inserted as a kind of appropriated quotation at the end of the stanza. The refrain is supposed to preexist the stanza.

Let us take a pastourelle as an example. The poet tells how, riding alone in the countryside, he met a young beauty who, upon seeing him, began to sing: "Nus ne doit lès le bois aler / Sans sa conpaignete" (no one should go into the woods / without his sweetheart). This is the refrain that ends the first stanza. Encouraged, the knight is so forward that he frightens the young woman. Refrain of the second stanza: "N'atouchiés pas a mon chainse, / Sir chevalier" (Do not touch my blouse, / sir knight).[2]

These two refrains appear elsewhere. They are thus doubly quotations—quotations of the words spoken by the character in the poem, which are themselves quotations of well-known refrains.

These refrains are generally borrowed from rondeaux. In the twelfth and thirteenth centuries, the rondeau was a brief dance song with a very simple form: a refrain of two lines on two rhymes, a couplet of three lines on the same two rhymes. The first line of the refrain is inserted after the first line of the stanza, and the entire refrain is repeated at the end (aAabAB). The scheme of the melody follows that of the rhyme ($\alpha\alpha\alpha\beta\alpha\beta$). The soloist sings the couplet, the chorus of dancers the refrain. It is not surprising that these refrains, which accompanied the dance, were on everyone's lips and in everyone's memory.

In addition, the rondeaux are themselves repetitive without ever being identical. Many (and, in particular, those cited by Jean Renart in *Guillaume de Dole*) endlessly evoke the lovely Aélis's morning ritual of rising and washing to make herself beautiful before going to dance in the meadow:

> Aaliz main se leva,
> *Bon jor ait qui mon cuer a!*

Biau se vesti et para
Desoz l'aunoi.
Bon jor ait qui mon cuer a:

N'est pas o moi.

Aélis arose very early—
Greetings to him who has my heart!

Dressed and adorned to look her best
under the alder tree.
Greetings to him who has my heart:

He is not with me.[3]

The variants are infinite, but the little scene is always the same. There is a kind of mirroring effect, of course, since the song being danced to itself evokes a scene of dancing. Sometimes there are even indications for the dance or allusions to the dance: "Remirez vos braz!" (Look at your arms!)—no doubt the dancers in a circle come closer together while extending their arms toward the inside, so that they do see them. Dancing and love are confused. The partner in the circle, to whom the young lady gives her hand, is her love, as Sylvie would say: "Ne fut plus loyalz amis / Que chilz que je tieng par la main" (There was never a love so faithful / as the one I held by the hand).

And while the soloist sings his few lines, which invite everyone to the dance and to love—"c'est tot la gieus, en mi les prez, . . . Dames i vont por caroler" (It's way over there in the meadows . . . Ladies go there to dance), male and female dancers, who express themselves in the refrain, are, as it were, moved by the song, by the lovely Aélis or the lovely Enmelot, surprised at her morning toilette or by the arrival of the awaited sweetheart: "Par ci passe li bruns, li biaus Robins . . . / Par ci passe Robins li amorous, / Encore en est li herbages plus douz" (He passes this way, the dark, the handsome Robin / He passes this way, Robin the lover, / And here the grass is softer). How could these familiar refrains, bearing memories of dancing and love and which are an emotion-filled commentary on the stanza, not come to everyone's lips?[4]

But it is always an interrupted commentary: just a line, which itself interrupts the couplet and remains in suspense, in expectation of its repetition and of the second line that will complete it. The rondeau has only five lines in all, and it is nothing but a succession of interruptions. We have insisted at great length on the role played by quotation and of the fragment in producing an impression of temporal depth, a surging forth from oblivion. And now the little genre of the rondeau, the most common, the most simple lyric form of its time, the genre most intimately connected to conviviality, to aesthetics, to the eroticism of dance, that genre plays on all these effects in a way both lighthearted and massive.

All that nearly leads us back to Marot, with whom we more or less began. Having moved from the sixteenth to the twentieth century, then back to the Middle Ages, are we not, in fact, in the process of closing the circle of time? I am not speaking here of Marot's rondeaux, which conform to the model of the rondeau from the end of the Middle Ages, which is slightly different from the dance rondeau we have described. But in the epigram *J'ay une lettre entre toutes eslite*, the allusion to the song *Allegez moy, doulce, plaisant brunette*, which is itself a rondeau, and the quotation of the line that is its refrain repeat in a different atmosphere and context the practice of the inserted refrain, the appropriated quotation, the commentary integrated into the poem and distinguished from it. And it does all that briefly: eight lines in Marot, five in a rondeau.

Brevity is so essential to the rondeau that it imposes an additional interruption, an interruption in the narration. The lovely Aélis's day is never pursued beyond her morning toilette. Should a trouvère—Baude de la Quarière—elaborate the rondeau and make an entire song from it, he nonetheless does not proceed any further in the outline of the story.[5] He gives a sort of depth or thickness to the five lines of the rondeau without going on. Each of the five stanzas of his song opens with a line from the rondeau, which is thus cited in its entirety, and the rest of the stanza is made up of a montage or potpourri of refrains. In the rondeau in its usual form, the story of the lovely Aélis, hardly outlined, is interrupted by the commentary of the refrain it inspires. In the same way, in Baude's song, elaborating on the story consists not in continuing it, in resolving the suspense, but in maintaining that suspense, charging every line with its weight of commentary. The refrains attach themselves to it in echoes of love, morning, springtime, and joy.

These accumulated refrains press from every corner of the memory. They emerge from the memory, but they are grasped only in their new context and in the present moment of the dance. The refrain is a quotation and an allusion. It thus belongs to the past. But it appears only in the novelty and freshness of the dance being danced, on which it comments. It is perpetually a revived old song. That is why, by its very nature, it puts the emphasis on the opposition and complementarity between old songs and new songs.

To comment on this essential couple of medieval poetics, we must again take up the question of the use of the word *antiquus* in the Middle Ages and of the opposition between "ancient" and "modern." There is a vast body of literature by theologians, philosophers, and historians on that question.[6] To remain within the field of letters, we may simply observe with Curtius that beginning in late Antiquity "classical" writers were always "ancient" writers.[7] There were no modern classics: "Cohors antiquior vel oratorume vel poetarum" (the very ancient cohort of orators or poets), writes Aulus Gellius. Even though the comparative *antiquior* has the banal meaning of "rather ancient," "very ancient," and is nothing but a kind of attenuated superlative, we may be allowed in spite of everything to point out its use. It is as if the admirable writer was always the one who was older—older than oneself. Membership in the cohort is a relative question with respect to the present, a question of comparison. We might add that *modernus*, which appeared in the sixth century, is derived from *modo*, on the model of *hodierunus* in relation to *hodie*. Literally, *modernus* applies more to the immediate past than to the present strictly speaking (*modo*, "recently," "a moment ago"). In that sense, the *moderni* would be immediate predecessors more than exact contemporaries. As for *novus*, which for its part does designate the immediacy of the present, it is rarely used in a literary context. The word applies in a privileged way to the New Testament, the New Covenant, to the definitive and perpetual novelty of Christ: "Et antiquum documentum / Novo cedat ritui."

In the field of letters, the primacy of the ancient was absolute, and only what came before was worthy of admiration. And yet, in the vernacular languages, the songs claimed to be new. "I am going to make a new song" is, in that and similar forms, a very frequent incipit, so frequent that it is hardly new. Moreover—and this has been observed often enough—all these songs resemble one another. Where is their novelty? In the *faire*, the making: "I am going *to make* a new song." The song is new not because it does not resemble the others that preceded it; it is new because it has just blossomed, because it is fresh. In the sincerity consistently asserted in this form of lyricism,[8] the new song is the one that has just bloomed as the result of a living feeling, not a withered, faded, or wilted song—wilted the way blooms wilt. I have not chosen that vegetal comparison at random. It is obligatory. It is suggested by the meteorological considerations that accompany the expression "new little song" in the pretty and famous song attributed to William IX, the first troubadour:

> Farai chansoneta nueva
> Ans que veut ni gel ni plueva.[9]

> I shall make a new little song
> Before the wind blows, or it freezes, or rains.

Elsewhere, it is explicit:

> L'estoc est plus vert que verdure,
> Qui nouvelleté nous figure,
> Et quant une fleur est nouvelle,
> Elle est communement plus belle
> Qu'elle n'est quant est marcie
> Et de sa couleur amenrie.[10]

> The stalk, greener than the greenery itself,
> Is for us the image of newness.
> And when a flower is new,

It is generally more beautiful
Than it is when it is wilted
And its color has passed away.

We are familiar with the description of Lanval's lady friend in
Marie de France's lai:

Flur de lis e rose nuvele
Quant ele pert el tens d'esté
Trespassot ele de bealté.

The lily and the young rose
when they appear in the springtime
are surpassed by her beauty.[11]

And in a half-allegorical, half-fantastic song of spring renewal, in
which young girls feed the poet's horse flowers:

Une pucellete
Avenans et bele
Li porte a maingier
Flurs et violetes,
E rozes nouvelles
Sus un eschaiquier.[12]

A little maiden
Pretty and charming
Brings it to eat
Flowers and violets
And new roses
On a chessboard.

The newness of the song, which is nothing other than the freshness of the feeling and of its expression, is thus a requirement in the
order of poetry and in that of love. Think only of the *Vita nuova*, of
the *dolce stil nuovo*.

What use are old songs, then? Some songs embrace that characteristic nonetheless, not only in the margins of the *grand chant courtois*, which we are particularly exploring here, but even among the

troubadours: "Lo vers comenssa / A son veil, sen antic (The poem begins / with an old melody, an old thought).[13]

Think of the biography of Cercamon, a contemporary of Marcabru's, the author of the above lines, and like him one of the first troubadours in the first half of the twelfth century: "Trobet vers e pastoretas / a la usanza antiga" (He composed poems and pastourelles / in the ancient manner).[14]

Is there not something like an anticipatory echo here of what a century after Cercamon (but no doubt a few years before the compilation of that biography) Jean Renart, in *Guillaume de Dole*, has Liénor's mother say regarding the *chansons de toile*, and which we recall one last time:

> Biaus filz, ce fu ça en arriers
> Que les dames et les roïnes
> Soloient fere lor cortines
> Et chanter les chançons d'istoire![15]

> My dear son, ladies and queens
> of days gone by
> were always singing spinning songs
> as they embroidered!

If we consider these examples briefly, we see that the scathing and paradoxical poet Marcabru boasts of composing a song in the ancient manner, not a new song: not "I am going to make a new song," but "The poem begins with an old melody, an old thought." He claims poetic antiquity for moral reasons. The theme of his song is that everything is backward: The rich are misers, the villeins behind their carts are courtly, the just claim to be sinners, youth is drowsy, joy fades, wickedness triumphs, sons degenerate. The only shining thing in the middle of this universal disaster is the praise of love. It is natural that a song that denounces the decadence of its age should lay claim to antiquity and cling to the past. It is natural that a polemical song should be sung to a *son veil*, an ancient melody, an old tune, already known, familiar, easy to remember: That has always been a way to facilitate the diffusion of songs of polemical or satirical character.

It is natural that his *sens*, that is, reason, reflection, the type of thought that engenders discourse, is "ancient," since today, says the poet, folly is triumphant. In appearance, there is only a *laudatio temporis acti*, a regret for the good old days, and these moral considerations have poetic repercussions.[16] Nonetheless, the poetic considerations are quite present: The song begins with them, claims to be composed in the ancient manner, and boasts about it. Finally, in combining the poetic and the moral by conferring a moral quality on poetic antiquity, the poet suggests that the "ancient" poetic manner implies a kind of simplicity and rugged virtue, in opposition to the hypocritical contortions of today, which are like the perverse refinement of this backward world where the nobleman is villainous, the villein noble, and so on.

Our second example is the biography of Cercamon, which is even more telling when we compare it with—or follow it by—the biography of another troubadour, Peire de Valeira. We know that these biographies, these lives in prose—*vidas*—of the troubadours served as an introduction to their poems in the manuscripts in which they were collected in anthology form at the end of the thirteenth century and during the fourteenth. Cercamon's biography plays on the combination of fascination and derision which old poetry inspires, in a manner somewhat similar to what we saw in Jean Renart's use of the *chansons de toile*. Let us cite it again, and this time in its entirety—it is very brief: "Cercamons si fo uns joglars de Gascoingna, et trobet vers e pastoretas a la usanza antiga. E cerquet tot lo mon lai on el poc anar, et per so fez se dire Cercamons" (Cercamon was a jongleur from Gascony, and he composed poems and pastourelles in the ancient manner. He traveled throughout the world, everywhere he could go, and that is why he took the name Cercamon ["world-seeker"]).

A poor jongleur whose self-mocking nickname makes it clear he is a vagabond. Poems in the manner of days gone by. There is something depreciative and probably humorous in the laconism of that *vida*, which is confirmed by that of the obscure Peire de Valeira: "Peire de Valeria si fo de Gascoingna, de la terra N'Arnaut Guillem de Marsan. Joglars fo el temps e en la sason que fo Marcabrus; e fez vers tals com hom fazia adoncs, de paubra valor, de foillas e de flors e de cans d'ausels. Sei cantar non aguen gran valor, ni el" (Pierre de Valeira was from Gascony, from the land of Lord Arnaut Guillem de Marsan. He was a jongleur of the time and season of Marcabru: he made poems as one did at the time, with little worth, about leaves, flowers, and birdsong. His songs did not have great worth, nor he either).[17]

There again, the biography affects a disdain, made mordant by the laconism and by the play on words contained in the expression "of the time and season of Marcabru." The time of Marcabru means simply his era, but since his outmoded poetry inspired by the renewal of springtime is cause for complaint, the biographer adds the word "season."[18] The *vida* presents and condemns the man and the work with amusing brevity. It has only disdain for the jongleur of long ago who belonged to the first generation of troubadours, the author of wretched little poems such as were written in his time, with springtime stanzas. As it happens, however, neither of the two poems by Peire de Valeira included after his *vida* contains a stanza on springtime. Alfred Jeanroy, grounding his judgment on these two short pieces of two stanzas, on these four *coblas*, which he published, judged their author much more recent than his biographer claimed.[19] That biographer therefore attributed a false antiquity to the poet; that attribution was certainly depreciative, but at the same time it awakened amusement and curiosity.

All that puts us on the trail of false old songs. After all, Marcabru had just composed his when he underscored its old melody and ancient *sens*. But false old songs, which for that very reason are moving or amusing—like the *chansons de toile*, like the songs of Cercamon or Peire de Valeira—lead one to imagine, to think about, to reflect on the mores of the time. That is the case with Marcabru's song. Thus, while medievalists look for signs of antiquity in medieval songs as support for their belief in the existence of even older and lost songs, medieval poets practiced both the affectation of novelty—my song is new, I shall make a new song, it is very fresh, fresh as love, fresh as the rose—and the affectation of antiquity. In short, they played with the idea of old songs and of new songs.

The Songs of the Fifteenth Century and Their Dissonant Echo

Let us return to the association between popular songs and old songs. Even if medievalists believed the popular song older than courtly lyricism and concealed by it, they very soon came to maintain that it had reemerged at the end of the Middle Ages and that the phenomenon was significant. The first volume published by the Société des Anciens Textes Français (Society of Old French Texts) was the *Chansons du XVe siècle* (1875), edited by Gaston Paris. We have already spoken of these collections of French songs that flourished beginning in the second half of the fifteenth century and throughout the following century. Often, and for a long time, they were designated as popular songs and were read as such; at the very least, the traces of a popular poetry were sought in them. And it is very true that certain of these songs have been conserved by the oral tradition until our own time. It is also true that they mark the decline of polyphony and the return to monody observed in the sixteenth century, and, in that respect, they may be said to use to advantage a certain simplicity.

The oldest and best known of these collections are those conserved in two manuscripts, called respectively the Paris and the Bayeux manuscripts.[20] These manuscripts in themselves, however, are not at all popular. They are very carefully prepared, and the Bayeux manuscript is even sumptuous. In what way are the songs they contain popular?[21] Formally, although certain of them illustrate what Conrad Laforte calls the "song in laisses,"[22] many are made to fit the fixed forms dear to the learned poetry of their time, the rondeau and, above all, the virelay (though it is true the virelay is both more supple and more elaborate). They are close to songs contemporary to them, which sustain the polyphonies of the Burgundian court. They are sometimes identical, though Burgundy musicians often composed new melodies for them. Hence the rondeau "Triste plaisir et doulou-reuse joye" (Bayeux 73)—which already appears in the *Canonici misc. 213* manuscript at the Bodleian Library in Oxford, dating from the first half of the fifteenth century—was put to music by Gilles Binchois even before it was copied into the Bayeux manuscript, since Binchois died in 1460. The well-known song *La belle se siet au pié de la tour* (Bayeux 90), which enjoyed a great vogue until the seventeenth century, provided the third voice for a composition by Dufay, with an entirely different melody than that given in the Bayeux manuscript and which is found elsewhere. Josquin des Prés put to music *A Dieu mes amours, a Dieu vous commant* (Bayeux 83), the famous lament *A qui direlle sa pensée / La fille qui n'a poinct d'amy*, and *En l'ombre d'un buisonnet* (Bayeux 101), whose bawdy suggestiveness made for its success.[23] In the case of the Bayeux manuscript, in most cases "we do not have before us . . . original monodies designed to be sung by a single voice; the melodies are separate parts of compositions for several voices, or for one voice with instrumental accompaniment."[24]

Thematically, most of these songs are the very direct heirs of the poetry of the trouvères; poems of courtly inspiration (the incipit *Triste plaisir et douloureuse joye* is in itself an emblem of this); pastourelles; aubades; *chansons de malmariée.*

What, then, led to their being defined as popular songs? Gaston Paris, who did not doubt they were popular, does not explain himself directly on this point in his introduction. But the description he gives of them has the value of argument:

> Nevertheless, these old songs are not of interest only to the historian or philologist. Several of them contain exquisite traits of naive grace, of delicate sentiment, of lighthearted and fine poetry, and above all, possess the inexpressible charm proper to the popular muse, the inimitable turn of thought, of feeling, and of revery, which defies analysis and sometime even clear understanding, but which moves the heart or imagination so keenly by its very unexpectedness. Others cut to the quick with a colorful coarseness, presenting the mores and manner of feeling of vanished ages: they are all the more interesting in that they usually originated among the most animated classes of a society that was so picturesque at the time. Others show us the impression produced on the nation by the great events of the time. All have the merit and incomparable value of being the faithful and spontaneous expression of French

genius, and of rendering for us traits, several of which seem to have disappeared, others of which are indelible, but all of which belong to the most intimate physiognomy of our people.[25]

Let us look at these considerations in reverse order. All these songs, concludes Gaston Paris, are "the faithful and spontaneous expression of French genius" and reflect the deep traits, some disappeared, others permanent, of the people of France. This is romantic thought in its purest form, upon which Gaston Paris was still basing himself in 1875. Popular productions, those of the Middle Ages and those of the modern era, are the spontaneous expression of national genius. But these songs, which all display that characteristic, are, according to Gaston Paris, divided into three categories. Let us continue in reverse order. Some are the echo of historical events. Why does Gaston Paris not consider them of interest to the historian, an interest he set aside at the beginning? Implicitly, but obviously if we refer to the lines that follow, because in his view that echo reflects the reaction of popular and national genius to events of national importance. This is a kind of extension, fundamentally natural, of his cantilena theory. In the mind or imagination of Gaston Paris, the cantilenas are lyric-narrative poems, and if he had achieved Benedetto Croce's level of thought, he might have said that all poetry is lyric. Here, the song is the cry that the event wrests from the people. La Villemarqué sought the echo of that cry in Breton songs.

A second category of songs consists of those that reflect the mores of the people. Here again, the historian ought to be interested. But Gaston Paris still has the people in view, insofar as they constitute an aesthetic category. All the same, the notion of "people" is not applied here to the national community as a whole but to the popular classes, to what he nicely calls "the most animated classes of society." Here is an example of the frequent slippage analyzed above between a national definition of the people and a social definition.

But the songs first signaled by Gaston Paris he defines in a different way, solely as a function of their manner and poetic effect, the manner and effect of the "popular muse." The term is not explained here or elsewhere, but we understand that it applies to a simple art, hardly conscious of its procedures, as opposed to a learned art. The nature and effects of that art are evoked, felicitously of course, but in a hazy manner, since what is at stake is an "inexpressible charm." It nonetheless appears that that charm lies precisely in a certain haziness, an indecisiveness of meaning, a looseness in logic. Such are the traits that signal "the popular muse." Such are also the traits that first struck Gaston Paris, those he signals first, and to which he in fact returns in a note that accompanies song 117.[26] It was these traits, or rather the impression they produced on him, that obviously led him to consider these songs popular. It is because of these traits that classification occurs around the notion of the popular, rather than the popular constituting simply a first category of that classification. It is these traits that elicit the final consideration on the "faithful and spontaneous expression of French genius." That theory, already out of date at the time, was clearly not the essential thing for Gaston Paris. He alludes to it only in the heat of his discussion and stylistic amplification. What is foremost in his eyes, what is the mark of popular poetry, is an aesthetics of rupture, of haziness, of suspense, of indecision. It is the impression produced by that aesthetics which leads him to consider these songs popular.

Fifty years later, Théodore Gérold does not call that popular character into question; it is confirmed in his eyes by the fact that many pieces have survived to our time. But he associates it with different traits. First, with a phenomenon of musical fashion. For him, these popular songs were conserved in lovely manuscripts because their melodies enjoyed a certain fashion. At the end of the Middle Ages, he writes, "ungainly and stilted compositions sometimes gave way to lively and appealing melodies." And he adds: "There is reason to observe that these poems of rather popular character are found especially in the collections with music; a great number of texts of songs would not have reached us if they had not been used in musical compositions that were a success."[27]

The new uses to which these songs were put by court musicians thus do not in any way belie their popular character; they simply show the vogue for them among a blasé audience hungry for freshness and simplicity.

In addition, in applying an analogous argument to the texts of these songs, Gérold is sensitive to their simplicity, which contrasts with the complexity of the learned poetry characteristic of the end of the Middle Ages and manifests itself in their style, the use they make of proverbs, and their use of assonance. But he is also sensitive to the fact that they are the direct heirs of the poetry of the trouvères:

> In some ways, the fifteenth-century song is linked to the art of the trouvères; the agreeable and lighthearted character and simple form of certain romances, pastourelles, and dance songs of the thirteenth century live again in it. The lyric pieces used by Machaut and his school in the fifteenth century—the lai, the lament, the *chanson roial*, the ballad, the virelay, the rondeau—are almost all much more complex and more learned in composition.[28]

These songs would thus be experienced as popular songs because their agreeable simplicity links them to the art of the trouvères. That intuition, in not being analyzed, leads to formulations that are at first sight surprising. First, the art of the trouvères is not particularly noted for its agreeable simplicity. Gérold, it is true, does not have in mind what we now call the *grand chant courtois*, but rather the noncourtly genres. Even so, and this is the second surprising point, these genres, which almost always include a refrain, are the closest thing to the fixed forms cultivated by the learned lyricism characteristic of the end of the Middle Ages. Of them, Gérold cites, as he ought, the rondeau. But in the thirteenth century, the rondeau was also the most simple form of the dance song. Later, Gérold observes that song 82, which is a rondeau of several stanzas, is "a rondelet of popular character." And he adds: "M. Jeanroy has demonstrated that in the rondelet the couplet is limited to two lines, and that, in addition, one of these two lines is repeated from the preceding couplet. That enjambment of one couplet on another is a trait characteristic of the popular song."[29]

Thus the fixed forms define both a learned lyricism and a popular lyricism. Let us add that Gérold could not have failed to find popular characteristics in this song 82, *Vecy le may, le joly mois de mai qui nous demeine. Au jardin mon pere entrai.* For that song, like its other versions—for example, song 8 of the Paris manuscript and, in the preceding century, songs 8 and 21 of the very interesting Florence collection[30]—are the ancestors of the song *J'ai descendu dans mon jardin* known by every child in France and felt to be the very prototype of the popular song.

Thus, everything gets mixed up together. The lyric forms of the thirteenth century may be invoked to account either for the poetry reputed to be learned or for the poetry reputed to be popular at the end of the Middle Ages. The songs of the fifteenth century may be considered popular precisely because they inspired court musicians but also because they were introduced into the repertoire of farces or stemmed from it. In the midst of all that, according to Gaston Paris and the less skillful Gérold, what appears most solid is what stems, not from fact, but from impression. For both authors, these songs consistently exude an impression of simplicity, of indifference to coherence and logic, of rootedness in an old tradition.

One cannot deduce a fact from an impression: for example, the fact that these songs are really popular, in whatever sense one gives to the word. For on this account, what produces more of an impression of naivete, of archaism, of unresolved suspense, than certain rondeaux by Christine de Pizan: *Il me semble qu'il a cent ans / Que mon amy de moi parti* (It seems to me it has been a hundred years / Since my sweetheart took leave of me). If one of these rondeaux were to slip into our collections, we would cite it as an example of a popular art that rings true. Moreover, as is only fair in the end, Max-Pol Fouchet, in his famous thematic anthology of French poetry, attributes to Christine the song *A qui direlle sa pensee / La fille qui n'a point d'ami* (To whom will she tell her thoughts / The girl who has no sweetheart). And he is not so culpable after all, not only because of its thematic resemblance to *Seulette suy et seulette demeure* (Lonely am I and lonely remain) but also because Christine herself does a pastiche of the popular *stornelli* ("Je vous vends la passerose, / Belle, à dire ne vous ose / Comment amour vers vous me tire; / Si l'apercevez tout sans dire"; I will sell you the primrose, / Darling, I dare not tell you / How love draws me to you; / If you see all without saying so). Does not Charles d'Orléans paraphrase street cries ("Petit mercier, petit panier")? Is he not interested in the rites of traditional celebrations ("Quant j'ay ouy le tabourin / Sonner pour s'en aller au may")? Is he not a lover of proverbs ("De legier pleure a qui la lippe pent")?

We cannot deduce a positive, historical fact from an impression, but we can deduce the existence of an aesthetic effect that *is* solid and real, more solid and more real than all the hypotheses of literary history, since it is very true that it produces that impression. The act of identifying certain songs as popular inevitably encounters uncertainties of fact and problems of definition that are nearly insoluble. In contrast, the fact that certain poetic traits regularly call forth the adjective "popular" is beyond doubt, and it is therefore from that point we must begin. The impression formulated by Gaston Paris and Théodore Gérold had been expressed innumerable times since the dawn of romanticism and even before. Here is a slightly more recent expression of it, which I take the liberty of citing because it brings together all these traits and because it is particularly clear, elegant, sensitive, and penetrating. It is taken from the preface by Henri Davenson, that is, Henri-Irénée Marrou, to his *Livre des chansons*:

> In our songs we loved the archaism, the awkwardness, the unintentional clumsiness, the improprieties of expression we attribute to "naivete," and even the dilapidated state in which these texts have sometimes come down to us, mutilated or deformed by the oral tradition. It happens that the lacunae, the holes in the sequence of ideas, engender ill-coordinated associations of ideas that leave an odd impression of irrationality, the fantastic, poetic mystery.[31]

Archaism, awkwardness, improprieties, dilapidation: These are the bases for the poetic charm of these songs. But, though we can see very well that the last three terms go together, why is the first associated with them? And do the last three terms really go together? In Marrou's view, awkwardness and improprieties of expression are obviously the unintentional counterpart to Verlainian "mistakes" and "indecisiveness." The most refined poetic art has shown that charm and even resonance of meaning can originate in the inadequation between the idea and its expression. The fact that that inadequation is unintentional, natural, "naive," makes the effect even stronger.

But who is to say it is unintentional? Is not accepting that without discussion betraying the relics of a romantic presupposition, of a faith in a spontaneous art little aware of its procedures, originating in the collective recesses of the people? And is not Marrou the victim of a vicious circle when he defines these songs as popular because their awkwardness is unintentional, and assumes that this awkwardness is unintentional because they are popular songs? In fact, he advances, at least implicitly, an argument in favor of this unintentional character by associating the state of dilapidation of these "texts, mutilated or deformed by the oral tradition," with the other traits. This characteristic has no apparent relation to awkwardness or improprieties of expression. But it leads to the same result, a lapse in logic, and it exerts the same charm on us. Since it is an accidental trait, the suggestion is that if the deformations due to the transmission of songs are unintentional, then the clumsiness of their composition may be as well, with both leading to the same poetic effect.

Might we, however, adopt Marrou's intuition but put aside the notion of "unintentional" and the distinction between incoherencies that can be traced back to the composition of the song and others that have to do with a defective transmission? For in both cases, we are in the realm of undemonstrable hypotheses: How can we know if an effect is intentional or not? Can there truly be an original, fixed version at the source of such songs? Is it not contradictory to suppose that such a version existed before it was corrupted at the time of its transmission, and to simultaneously grant that from its origin the text may have displayed incoherencies? Is not the first of these suppositions the vestige of Gaston Paris's theory, whose aim was to restore a so-called primitive version by applying the methods of the critical edition to popular songs—a theory whose application by Gilliéron to the example of *A la claire fontaine*, in the admission of the author himself, was not conclusive?[32] Conversely, if we give up the futile hope of going back to an original state of these songs; if we refrain even from seeking which incoherencies may be original and which others may have to do with transmission and focus exclusively on the effect they produced and the attraction they exerted when the song was transcribed; in short, if we consider the notions of archaism, awkwardness, and mutilation in themselves, we see that they are joined together and proceed from one another on the basis of that last characteristic, mutilation.

We are then back to the proposition I formulated in my inaugural lecture. Everything rests on the impression that the text as we know it is mutilated, in tatters, fragmentary. That impression entails awkwardness: The text is incoherent. It entails, at least in part, archaism: The fragment appears to be a relic of a disappeared whole. But it also entails quotation: The fragment in its discontinuity is, as it were, within brackets, inserted within a context from which it detaches itself, the context of a culture on which it produces the effect of awkwardness and of archaism, effects that cannot exist except in the gaze the culture casts on them. Thus, in every era, the system of relations and oppositions which structures literary representations requires that certain productions be laden with these effects in the eyes of official culture, that they contrast with that culture even while being exhibited within it. Whatever the reality or illusion of their antiquity, whatever the reality or illusion of their awkwardness, of their rusticity, whatever the reality or artifice of their fragmentation, they are invited to occupy the place assigned to them within the literary landscape.

Let us return to the songs of the fifteenth century. The impressionist description given by Gaston Paris, broadened and confirmed by the analysis of Marrou; the echo Paris believed he heard of the life and reaction of the popular classes of society, and singularly from the rustic world, as he notes in a rightly famous passage from his introduction to the edition of the Paris manuscript;[33] the set of remarks made by Gérold on their simplicity, their direct relation to the poetry of the trouvères, the attraction they exerted on court musicians, and the use they made of them: All these observations converge and agree. From these songs and their incoherencies a coherent image emerged, consistent with the interpretation proposed here. These songs were collected to balance out the stilted aridity of the learned poetry of their time, by giving the impression of a refreshing plunge into a rustic universe, presented as the bearer of ancient traditions.

It would be easy to multiply examples of that situation and to elaborate our commentary on it, if we were not afraid of wearying of it. It would be easy to point out the tiny linguistic traits, already obsolete at the end of the fifteenth century but which persisted in the popular song, to the point of becoming among its distinctive traits: invariability of the epicene adjective in the masculine and feminine, suppression of the pronoun subject. It would be easy to observe, as Gérold does, types of refrain or repetitions of lines (the first or last of the stanza, the last line of the stanza repeated at the beginning of the next), unknown in the fixed forms of learned lyricism, at least in France, but which were later common in popular songs and whose presence in other lyric domains, for example, in the Gallician Portuguese *cantigas d'amigo*, may reveal a long life on the margins. Inventors of French songs were not content to take up the themes and manner of the poetry of the trouvères. They modified them so as to give them a kind of country patina, and that innovation had a conservative value, since it contributed toward casting them even farther from the universe of court poetry. Should one find a pastourelle, its virtuous shepherdess refuses to pay with her person the knight who protected her sheep from the wolf (Paris 29). The insistence on that virtue, the threat of the wolf, which expresses a preoccupation on the part of the shepherdess and not on the part of the seducer, the ambiguity of the threat itself, which would later be humorously expressed in the morality play in verse *Le petit chaperon rouge* (Little Red Riding Hood)[34] and which, as a metaphor of feminine terror and desire, contributed toward making it a woman's song and thus something to be cast away into the universe of the shepherdess: Everything tends to introduce a shift in the old genre in such a way as to root it in the rusticity it originally mocked. In addition, that piece is the ancestor of the popular song—"popular" in the stereotypical sense of the expression—*Mon père avait cinq cents moutons.*

Women's songs were particularly common and, as has always been the case, were sometimes combined with the theme of dawn (Paris 30), the morning activities upon rising, the visit to the garden, or the bird as counselor (Paris 99, 76, 104). Hence there is a marked predilection for the form that, already at the time of the trouvères, was opposed to other forms by its coloration of antiquated simplicity. Even more significant, however, is the treatment of the courtly legacy itself. The pieces that most directly concentrate the inspiration and manner of the *grand chant courtois* sometimes create a greater impression than the others of being somehow borrowed or dressed up. The overture to springtime, the floral metaphors, the lover's lament are pretexts for somewhat clumsy, somewhat uncouth affectations, putting forward tired stereotypes, playing on social distance, on rusticity, to emphasize temporal distance—the obsolescence of courtly themes and motifs: *Plaisante fleur que j'ay tant desiree* (Paris 37), *Plaisante fleur gente et jolie* (Bayeux 96), *Reine des fleurs que j'ai tant desiree* (Paris 55, Bayeux 4 and 19), *Fleur de gaité, donnez-moy joye* (Bayeux 30), *Fleur de gaieté, allegés le martire* (Bayeux 31), *Réconfortés le petit cueur de moy* (Paris 54, Bayeux 21).

And in fact, as we have suggested, the most consistent and most symptomatic trait is distance, dissonance, incoherence, whether in tone, language register, thematics, or continuity. There is an impression of incompletion, as in *Jamés d'amoureux couart n'orrés bien dire* (Paris 78). There are ill-timed leaps from the young lady's words to those of the lover, as in the *chanson de malmariée Je feusse resjouye* (Paris 79) or in *Nous estions trois jeunes fillettes / Qui toutes trois avions amy* (Paris 117), whose beginning is close to the thirteenth-century song *Trois sereurs sus rive mer / Chantent cler* and which proceeds to the well-known parallel between the rich suitor and the poor true love. There is a drifting in the imagination, as in the lovely woman's song *Que faire s'amour me laisse? / Nuit et jour ne puis dormir* (Paris

99), which wanders off into an evocation of a beautiful ship, similar to that in the later *Filles de La Rochelle*. Finally, there is the total disjointedness of the counting rhymes, such as *Della rivière sont / Les troys gentes demoiselles* (Paris 136), which combine an ancestor of sorts to the children's song *Ainsi font, font, font / Les petites marionnettes* and a counting rhyme that still exists:

> Della rivière sont
> Les troyes gentes damoiselles;
> Della rivière sont:
> Font ung sault et puys s'en vont.

> Je perdy assoir ycy
> Je perdy assoir icy
> Le bonnet de mon amy
> Le bonnet de mon amy

> "Et vous l'avez."
> "Et vous mentez."
> "Et qui l'a donc?"
> "Nous ne savon."

> Della rivière sont
> Les troys gentes damoiselles;
> Della rivière sont,
> Font ung sault and puis s'en vont.

> From the river are
> The three gentle maidens;
> From the river are:
> They leap and go away.

> I lost here last night
> I lost here last night
> My sweetheart's bonnet
> My sweetheart's bonnet

> "And you have it."
> "And you are lying."
> "And who has it then?"
> "We do not know."

From the river are
The three gentle maidens;
From the river are:
They leap and go away.

And what are we to say about the bizarre and almost surrealist song *Fillettes de Montfort*:

Les fillettes de Montfort,
Ils ont trouvé en leur voye
Ung cheval qui estoit mort.

Sir don Dieu dondaine
Va, sire donde,
Sire don Dieu, ho, hu, hayne,
Ha, huri, ha,

Hé! Hauvoy!
Sur la mer quant il vente
Il y faict dangereux aller.[35]

The little girls from Montfort,
Found along their way
A horse that was dead.

Lord Don God dondaine,
God, lord donde
Lord don God, ho, hu, hane,
Ha, hury, ha,

Hey! Havoy!
Upon the sea when the wind blows
It is dangerous to go.

These dissonances, which in a certain manner only amplify the dissonance that the opposition between refrain and stanza has forever played on, are the basis of the quotation effect and of the impression that we are dealing with a collection of fragments. They are in line with an element we have not yet taken into account: the theatrical use of French songs, many of which are inserted into farces, but always as fragments in the form of quotations, punctuating the words spoken as refrains, in such a way as to both echo them and contrast with them.[36] Yet does not that contradict the hypothesis that these songs feign to be rooted in the past and posit themselves as foreign to the poetic fashions of their time? For if they were sung on the stage, it was because they were in fashion. But what is fashion? Novelty? More than that, no doubt, it is the repetition of what is supposed to be novelty, in such a way as to create a sort of saturation of the familiar. The song must be understood as a hit tune. Perhaps it dates from yesterday, but it is as if it has always been there, since everyone knows it. It is a kind of mocking aspect of tradition. Moreover, this was already an old effect in medieval theater. As we have already had occasion to underscore, at the end of *Jeu de la Feuillée*, when the drinkers in the tavern begin to sing in an inebriated voice, they sing *Aie se siet en haute tour* (line 1024), that is, a fragment of a *chanson de toile*, a type of song marked by signs of distance and obsolescence. And, this time without any mocking intention, it is also the timbre of a *chanson de toile* one hears in the Occitan play *Jeu de sainte Agnès*.[37] No, decidedly, the presence of these songs in farces only confirms their aesthetics of the swerve, a swerve grounded in the hypothesis of rootedness.

We have attempted to follow that swerve in all its mobile forms: broken refrains, quotations that, come from who knows where, run through your head and come to your lips. From who knows where? From the past, from the grandmothers, from the people, from childhood: that is what the song in the present instant, the only time when it resonates, relentlessly gives us to understand, gives us to hear. It is in bits and pieces, as if it were emerging in tatters from the mists of time and childhood. It is like the memories of early childhood conserved in the form of juxtaposed and fragmented images. It is a beginning never pursued but indefinitely amplified by the echo of revery, like the rondeau of the lovely Aélis, and like the song *Nous n'irons plus au bois / Les lauriers sont coupés*, as George Sand experienced it as a child:

> I remember another time, when we were dancing in a circle, that the same little girl sang:

Nous n'irons plus au bois,
Les lauriers sont coupés.

We shall go no more to the woods,
The laurel trees are cut down.

I had never been to the woods that I know of and perhaps had never seen laurel trees. But apparently I knew what they were, for these two little lines left me daydreaming for a long time. I withdrew from the dance to think about them, and fell into a great melancholy. I did not want to share my preoccupation with anyone, but I could have easily cried, I felt so sad and deprived of that charming laurel wood I had entered in a dream, only to be immediately dispossessed of it.[38]

This song must have a strange power: Nodier and Nerval both loved it; it inspired Banville to write a poem that, like its medieval ancestors, uses the effects of an inserted refrain and a refrain quotation;[39] and it provided Louis Hémon with the title for a novel (*La belle que voilà*).

Are the songs of the Middle Ages old songs? Some of them wanted to be, and, like "the fairy of legend," they have succeeded in being "eternally young," because they appear forever old. That is also the secret of the songs that, for no other reason, we call "popular."

Let us repeat one last time: It is oblivion that designates the past. These heady and distant songs must be lacunary, or their disjointedness must give the impression of a vestige, so that we may suppose them half effaced by time. All the collectors of folklore have the impression that they have arrived just a little too late. All their informers have the impression that songs and stories have been lost, that they have been lost recently, that a few bits and pieces of them still remain, but that it is their mothers who should have been questioned.[40] And each of us pursues within our memories the songs of our own vanished childhood. For a thousand years, and much longer no doubt, poetry has known that. Century after century, from Mozarabic *khardjas* to *chansons de toile* to French songs of the fifteenth century to the songs of the Valois dear to Nerval, poetry has brought itself into relief by profiling in the distance the half-effaced silhouette of another poetry, whose antiquity and simplicity counterbalance and confirm both its sophistication and its novelty. To do that, it takes care to arrange the trompe l'oeil perspective on the past through the play of ruptures and dissonances. For the future folklorist, it creates an object that may be illusory. It casts a shadowy light that it incessantly pretends to want to dissipate.

■ Notes

Inaugural Lecture

Published without notes in the collection "Leçons inaugurales," vol. 131 (Paris: Collège de France, 1995).

1. "I hope this story pleases young boys and girls; but, to tell the truth, I dare not hope so. It is too frivolous for them and fit only for children from the olden days. I have a pretty little neighbor of nine years old whose private library I examined the other day. I found many books on microscopes and zoophytes, as well as several scientific novels. I opened one of them and fell upon these lines: 'The cuttlefish, *Sepia officinalis*, is a cephalopod mollusk whose body contains a spongy organ with a cuttlebone frame similar to lime.' My pretty little neighbor finds this novel very interesting. I beg her to never read the story of Abeille, if she does not want to see me die of shame." Anatole France, *Abeille*, first published in *La Revue Bleue* (1882–83); reprinted in *Balthasar* (Paris: Calmann-Lévy, 1889), cited here from Anatole France, *Oeuvres*, edition established, presented, and annotated by Marie-Claire Bancquart (Paris: Gallimard, Bibliothèque de la Pléiade, 1984), 1:648. [Unless otherwise noted, quoted passages are my translation—*Trans.*]

2. "Qualunque piu scabroso argomento, trattato da lui, pareva aquistare chiarezza inaspettata, divenire capace d'interessare pus coloro che meno fossero a cio preparati." (When discussed by him, the most

difficult subject appeared to acquire an unexpected clarity, to be able to interest even those who were least prepared for it). Francesco Novati, *Gaston Paris*, in *A ricolta: Studi e profili* (Bergamo, 1907), 22; cited by Mario Mancini in his introduction to Alberto Limentani, *Alle origini della filologia romanza* (Parma: Pratiche Editrice, 1991), 19.

3. This passage, in which we see Sylvestre Bonnard reading an issue of *Romania*—a brand new journal at the time—and commenting on its spirit, is famous among medievalists: "I began to read a journal that, though directed by young people, is excellent. The style is rough, but the spirit zealous. The article I read surpasses in precision and resoluteness everything produced during my youth. The author of this article, M. Paul Meyer, marks each error with a sharp fingernail." *Le crime de Sylvestre Bonnard, membre de l'Institut* (Paris, 1881), cited from Anatole France, *Oeuvres*, 1:299.

4. "It is always with a joyous and virile emotion that one hears the singular and audacious words coming from the mouth of men of science who, purely from professional honor, come to speak the truth, a truth that concerns them only because it is the truth, which they have learned to cherish in their art. . . . Hence M. Paul Meyer, who no doubt was little concerned until then with Zola, and would not have troubled himself for a moment on his behalf, and who perhaps was the close friend of the minister of war, defended with joyful sympathy Zola, whom he recognized as being in the right, and opposed, to all the pressures, all the arguments of the military authority, a certain number of assertions regarding certain strokes, certain curves, to conclude: 'I swear that it cannot be Dreyfus's handwriting.' These words are moving to hear, for we feel they are simply the conclusion of a reasoning made in accordance with scientific rules and irrespective of any opinion on the affair." Marcel Proust, *Jean Santeuil*, edition established by Pierre Clarac, with the collaboration of Yves Sandre (Paris: Gallimard, Bibliothèque de la Pléiade, 1971), 649–50. See Alberto Limentani, "Paléographie, épopée et 'affaire Dreyfus.' Quelques remarques sur le thème: Paul Meyer et les chansons de geste," *Senefiance* 20–21 (1987): 815–42; reprinted in Italian under the title "Meyer, l'epopea e l'affaire Dreyfus,'" in *Alle origini della filologia romanza*, introduction by Mario Mancini (Parma: Pratiche Editrice, 1991), 123–44.

5. Joseph Bédier, *Le roman de Tristan et Iseut renouvelé*, preface by Gaston Paris (Paris: H. Piazza, 1900).

6. We see this, for example, in the enumeration of works interpreted

by the jongleurs at the wedding of Flamenca and Archambaud de Bourbon in the Occitan romance *Flamenca* (in *Les troubadours*, ed. and trans. René Lavaud and René Nelli [Paris: Desclée de Brouwer, 1960], 674–81, lines 593–709); in the bragging and follies of two rival jongleurs in the *dit* that depicts them (*Des deux bordeors ribauz*, ed. Anatole de Montaiglon and Gaston Raynaud, in *Recueil général des fabliaux*, [Paris, 1872], 1–12); and in certain kinds of vernacular *ars poetica*, the *ensenhamen* ("teachings"), for instance, in langue d'oc (see François Pirot, *Recherches sur les connaissances littéraires des troubadours occitans et catalans des XIIᵉ et XIIIᵉ siècles*, vol. 14, *Les "sirventes-ensenhamens" de Guerau de Cabrera, Guiraut de Calanson et Bertrand de Paris* (Barcelona: Memorias de la Real Academia de Buenas Letras de Barcelona, 1972).

7. "Cil qui fist d'Erec et d'Enide / Et les comandemenz Ovide / Et l'art d'amor en romanz mis / Et le mors de l'espaule fist, / Dou roi Marc et d'Iseut la Blonde, / Et de la hupe et de l'aronde / Et dou rousignol la muance / I. novel conte recomence"; "He who wrote of Erec and Enide, and translated into French the commands of Ovid and the Art of Love, and wrote the Shoulder Bite, and about King Mark and the fair Iseut, and about the metamorphosis of the Lapwing, the Swallow, and the Nightingale, will tell another story now." Chrétien de Troyes, *Cligès*, ed. and trans. by Charles Méla, in *Romans*, edited by Michel Zink (Paris: Le Livre de Poche, La Pochothèque, 1994), 291, lines 1–8; idem, *Arthurian Romances*, ed. and trans. by W. W. Comfort (New York: E. P. Dutton, 1935), 91.

8. See, in particular, Jörn Gruber, *Die Dialektik des Trobar: Untersuchungen zur Struktur und Entwicklung des occitanischen und französischen Minnesangs des 12. Jahrhunderts*, Beihefte zur Zeitschrift für Romanische Philologie 194 (Tübingen: Neimeyer, 1983).

9. For a rapid overview of that question, see Michel Stanesco and Michel Zink, *Histoire européenne du roman médiéval: Esquisse et perspectives* (Paris: PUF, 1992).

10. Vico, Herder, and Hegel took into consideration all the ages of civilization. Only Hegel attributed a decisive importance to the Middle Ages in themselves, as the first period of the "romantic" era, which is to say, the modern era. Both Vico, who in essence approached the Middle Ages through a reflection on Dante, and Herder—though to a lesser extent—were interested primarily in Antiquity and, in a sense, did no more than apply to the Middle Ages reflections suggested to them by the Homeric age and its poetry. One finds many later examples of that atti-

tude: The famous Lachmann method, which played such an important role in editions of medieval texts, was elaborated for editions of classical and biblical texts; it was as a specialist of Homeric poetry that Milman Parry became interested in Serbo-Croatian oral epics, which medievalists then linked to chansons de geste; and in the present essay, the reading of Homer by Pindar, as it was analyzed and interpreted by G. Nagy, will be invoked with reference to the place occupied by the chanson de geste within medieval poetry as a whole. Let us note finally that Vico was translated into French by Michelet and that Herder was translated by Quinet: That says something of their importance—and in a certain way their joint importance—for nineteenth-century French thought.

11. Thomas Percy published his *Reliques of English Poetry* in 1765, just when James Macpherson was working on his supposed translations of Ossian.

12. Jacob Grimm often gave the clearest expression to Herder's ideas, in such formulations as "das Volk dichtet" (the people create) or "jedes Epos muss sich selbst dichten" (every epic must create itself), or in his definition of popular poetry as nature poetry (*Naturpoesie*). See, among others, *Ueber die Wirkung der Dichtkunst auf die Sitten der Völker* (1778), in Johann Gottfried Herder, *Sämtliche Werke*, vol. 8, ed. B. Suphan (Hildesheim, 1967). Among the works of Herder translated into French, one finds elements leading in this direction in *Idées sur la philosophie de l'histoire de l'humanité: Livres choisis*, translated by Edgar Quinet, introduction, notes, and dossier by Marc Crépon (Paris: Presses Pocket, 1991).

13. In the two books of *Volkslieder* Herder published in 1778–79, borrowings from Percy and Ossian appear haphazardly with lyric poems from classical Greece, pieces by Catullus, Quinault, and Fénelon, Shakespearean sonnets, poems by Goethe, a song written by the trouvère Thibaud de Champagne, and so on. See Johann Gottfried Herder, *Werke*, vol. 3, ed. Ulrich Gaier (Frankfurt-am-Main: Deutscher Klassiker Verlag, 1990), 69–430.

14. See J.-A. Bizet, *La poésie populaire en Allemagne: Etude suivie d'un choix de "Volkslieder" avec traduction et notes* (Paris: Aubier, 1959).

15. The original title of this short story, at its first publication in the *Revue des Deux Mondes* (15 September 1869), was *Le manuscrit du professeur Wittembach* (The manuscript of Professor Wittembach).

16. Théodore Hersart de La Villemarqué, *Barzaz-Breiz: Chants populaires de la Bretagne recueillis et publiés avec une traduction française, des*

éclairissements, des notes et les mélodies originales (Paris, 1839; reprint, Paris: Librairie académique Perrin, 1959; and Maspéro, 1983).

17. The first part ("The Departure") of song 11, "Lez-Breiz," shows the astonishment of the child Les-Breiz when faced with a knight and reports their dialogue in terms that resemble a brief rustic transposition—sometimes almost verbatim—of the first episode of the *Conte du Graal* (lines 98–594). The second part, "The Return," has Lez-Breiz returning to the manor of his deceased mother to find his sister there: The passage corresponds to an episode from *The Second Continuation*, vol. 4 of *The Continuation of the Old French Perceval of Chrétien de Troyes*, ed. William Roach (Philadelphia: American Philosophical Society, 1971), lines 23598–703.

18. See, for example, on the second point, the first words of *Philosophie der Geschichte zur Bildung der Menschheit*, where Herder indicates that in pushing his investigations ever further into humanity's past, he became ever more convinced that it had emerged whole from a single source; this entailed linking himself to the original unity of earthly paradise. Johann Gottfried Herder, *Werke*, vol. 4, ed. Jürgen Brummack and Martin Bollacher (Frankfurt-am-Main: Deutscher Klassiker Verlag, 1994), 11. Cf. the analyses of Maurice Olender on Herder's thinking in *Les langues du paradis* (Paris: Le Seuil, 1994).

19. Martianus Capella, *De nuptiis Mercurii et Philologiae* (The wedding of Mercury and Philology). This erudite and humorous book from the beginning of the fifth century A.D., which consists in great part of a treatise on the seven liberal arts, was a great success in the Middle Ages and was used as a manual.

20. Autograph document belonging to M. Georges B. Alphandéry, Château de Brignan, Montfavet (Vaucluse), published by Daniel Poirion, "Un document inédit: Note de P. Paris demandant la création d'une chaire de littérature du Moyen Age," *Perspectives Médiévales* 2 (November 1976): 4–5.

21. On F. Diez, see Richard Baum, "Friedrich Diez," in *Romanistik: Eine Bonner Erfindung*, ed. Willi Hirdt (Bonn: Bouvier Verlag, 1993): *Teil I: Darstellung*, 45–140; and *Teil II: Dokumentation*, 457–913.

22. See Pierre von Moos, "Muratori et les origines du médiévisme italien," paper presented to the colloquium on Gaston Paris and the beginnings of medieval studies, organized by A. Boreau and H. Bloch (Cerisy-la-Salle, 23–30 July 1994), forthcoming in *Romania*.

23. Claude Fauchet (1530–1602), *premier président* of the Cour des Monnaies from 1581 until his death, published his *Recueil de l'origine de la langue et poesie françoise* in 1581 and his *Antiquitez gauloises et françoises* in 1599. Some consider him the best connoisseur of French literature of the Middle Ages before the development of modern philology. Du Cange, born in 1610, devoted the greater part of a life of prodigious hard work to his *Glossarium mediae et infimae Latinitatis*, three volumes in folio (first edition published in Paris in 1678). From 1733 to 1736, the Benedictines of Saint-Maur offered a very augmented edition in six volumes, to which the four-volume supplement by Dom Carpentier was added in 1768. A rewritten edition in seven volumes, the last of which includes a glossary of Old French as well as tables and appendixes, appeared between 1847 and 1850. The Du Cange edition frequently brings together, under the Latin term, examples in Old French borrowed from literature.

24. Jean-Baptiste La Curne de Sainte-Palaye (1697–1781), author of the first large dictionary of Old French, in 1759 brought together and published five essays he had read before the Académie des Inscriptions et Belles-Lettres between 1746 and 1750, under the title *Mémoires sur l'ancienne chevalerie considérée comme un établissement politique et militaire*. That work has been extremely influential.

25. The twenty-eight volumes of that periodical appeared between 1775 and 1789, under the direction of Marquis de Paulmy, Marquis de Bastide, and Count de Tressan.

26. François de Baculard d'Arnaud, *Sargines*, one of the short stories in *Les épreuves du sentiment* (Paris: Le Jay, 1722). "The name of the hero is borrowed from Joinville, who is abundantly cited in the notes, in addition to Monstrelet, Froissart, *Lancelot*, Sire de Coucy, Alain Chartier, Villehardouin, Thibaut de Champagne, Perceforest, but clearly less in toto than the inevitable Lacurne de Sainte Palaye." Roland Mortier, "Aspects du rêve chevaleresque de La Curne de Sainte-Palaye à Madame de Staël," in *Idéologie et propagande en France*, ed. Myriam Yardeni (Paris: Picard, 1987), 139. After the liberation of Saint Louis and his return to France, Geoffroy de Sergines defended with inadequate means the debris of the Eastern Roman kingdom. Rutebeuf, whom Baculard d'Arnaud did not know about (he situates the action of his short story during the reign of Philip Augustus), sings Geoffroy's praises on several occasions and devotes a *Complainte* to him.

Mme de Genlis, *Les Chevaliers du Cygne ou la Cour de Charlemagne* (Paris: Lemierre, 1795).

27. Parseval says he worked on this poem for more than twenty years. If the assertion is correct, and if this official poet of the empire who quickly went over to the Bourbons was not seeking to mask his political about-face under the continuity of his literary activity, his *Philippe Auguste* would have been undertaken at the time of Napoleon's plan to invade England from Boulogne-sur-Mer—the same England on which Parseval was casting aspersions in occasional poems written at about the same time.

28. Of course, Nerval chose the form of the rondeau to lament the disappearance of the "happy times of chivalry," "times of Arthurs and of Blioberis" ("O temps heureux de la chevalerie," in Gérard de Nerval, *Oeuvres complètes*, ed. Jean Guillaume and Claude Pichois [Paris: Gallimard, Bibliothèque de la Pléiade, 1989], 1:16). But this rondeau, irregular in form and in fact rather flat, has a mannered tone that in no way recalls the rondeaux of the Middle Ages.

29. Claude Fauriel himself, who was the most representative type of the romantic medievalist in France and a lover of popular song, felt little admiration for medieval romances and chansons de geste as poems, viewing them only as historical documents: "These songs or epic materials all belong to ages of ignorance and barbarism, of which they are for us the only documents and whose mores, beliefs, and civilization they faithfully represent. Hence the philosophical and historical interest attached to them." Course by Fauriel on "les romans chevaleresques" (chivalric romances), Bibliothèque de l'Institut de France, Fauriel collection, ms. 2348 (l-2), folio 274. We would no doubt find different points of view expressed in the other countries of Europe.

30. Gustave Flaubert, *La première Education sentimentale*, ed. Martine Bercot (Paris: Le Livre de Poche, 1993), 305–6.

31. Gaston Paris, *La poésie du moyen âge* (Paris: Hachette, 1885), preface, 1:ix and viii (1903 edition). See Ursula Bähler, "Notes sur l'acception du terme de philologie romane chez Gaston Paris," *Vox Romanica* 54 (1995): 27–28. I would like to thank U. Bähler for having allowed me to read this article before its publication. It was first presented as a paper at the Cerisy colloquium on Gaston Paris, 23–30 July 1994.

32. Gaston Paris, preface to *Chansons du XVᵉ siècle publiées d'après le manuscrit de la Bibliothèque Nationale de Paris* (Paris: SATF, 1875), v.

33. That conception appears most strikingly when Bédier defends the "precellence" of the Oxford manuscript of *La chanson de Roland* and celebrates Turold's genius in *La chanson de Roland commentée* (Paris: H. Pi-

azza, 1927). Bédier takes the view opposite to Gaston Paris's conceptions in *Les fabliaux: Etudes de littérature populaire et d'histoire littéraire du Moyen Age* (Paris: Champion, 1893), in which he denies that the fabliaux have an Indian origin, and in his great work *Les légendes épiques*, 4 vols. (Paris: Champion, 1908–13), in which he opposes the hypothesis that "cantilenas" from the Carolingian era could be at the origin of the chanson de geste.

34. "Genie ist eine Sammlung Naturkräfte: es kommt also auch aus dem Händen der Natur und muss vorausgehen, ehe Geschmack werden kann" (Genius is a union of natural forces: it thus comes from the hands of nature and must precede the appearance of taste). Johann Gottfried Herder, *Ursachen des gesunkenen Geschmacks bei den verschiedenen Völkern, da er geblühet*, competition of the Königl. Akademie der Wissenschaft for 1773, in Herder, *Werke*, 4:113.

35. The *khardjas*, accompanied by various translations that have been proposed for them, were published by Klaus Heger, *Die bisher veröffentlichen Hargas und ihre Deutungen* (Tübingen, 1960). For later bibliography, see Richard Hitchcock, *The Kharjas Research: Bibliographics and Checklists* (London: Grant and Cutler, 1977). On the question of the relation between the strophic form of the Arabo-Andalusian *muwwashah* and *zadjal* and Romance strophes, the best summaries are still those of Pierre Le Gentil, *Le virelai et le villancico: Le problème des origines arabes* (Paris: Les Belles Lettres, 1954), and idem, "La strophe zadjalesque, les khardjas et le problème des origines du lyrisme roman," *Romania* 84 (1963): 1–24, 209–50, 409–11. For a comparison of the *khardjas* with French refrains, Celtic lyric poetry, and classical and medieval Latin lyricism, see Peter Dronke, "Nuevas observaciones sobre las jaryas mozarabes," *Crotalón: Anuario de Filologia Española* 1 (1984): 99–114.

36. Michel Zink, *Les chansons de toile* (Paris: Champion, 1978).

37. "Biaus filz, ce fu ça en arriers / Que les dames et les roïnes / Soloient fere lor cortines / Et chanter les chançons d'istoire!" Jean Renart, *Roman de la rose ou de Guillaume de Dole*, ed. Félix Lecoy (Paris: Champion, CFMA, 1966), lines 1148–51; idem, *The Romance of the Rose or Guillaume de Dole*, trans. Patricia Terry and Nancy Vine Durling (Philadelphia: University of Pennsylvania Press, 1993), 33.

38. *Bele Aiglentine* (lines 2235–94), at least if I am right in attributing these characteristics to it. On this song, which will be discussed later on, see Paul Zumthor, *Essai de poétique médiévale* (Paris: Le Seuil, 1972), 164–66, 290–97.

39. Ms. Paris Bibl. Nat. Fr. fr. 12744, in G. Paris, *Chansons du XVᵉ siècle*, Ms. Paris Bibl. Nat. Fr. fr. 9346 (Bayeux manuscript), in Théodore Gérold, *Le manuscrit de Bayeux: Texte et musique d'un recueil de chansons du XVᵉ siècle* (Strasbourg: Public. de la Faculté des Lettres, 1921).

40. See Walter H. Kemp, *Burgundian Court Song in the Time of Binchois: The Anonymous "Chansons" of El Escorial, MS V.III.24* (Oxford: Clarendon Press, 1990).

41. *Les épigrammes*, book 3, no. 50, "J'ay une lettre entre toutes eslite ...," *Huictain*, in Clément Marot, *Oeuvres poétiques*, ed. Gérard Defaux (Paris: Classiques Garnier, 1993), 2:315–16.

42. Molière, *Le misanthrope*, in *Oeuvres complètes*, vol. 2, ed. Georges Couton (Paris: Gallimard, Bibliothèque de la Pléiade, 1971), lines 385–404.

43. *La nouvelle Héloïse*, pt. 5, letter 7, in Jean-Jacques Rousseau, *Oeuvres complètes*, ed. B. Guyon, J. Scherer, and C. Guyot (Paris: Gallimard, Bibliothèque de la Pléiade, 1961), 2:609.

44. We see this, of course, in *Chansons et légendes du Valois* but also in *Sylvie* and especially in *Angélique*, where quotations of songs in the form of fleeting digressions are accompaniments to the evanescent story of Abbot de Bucquoy, the story that ought to be the subject of the narrative and the quest for which ends in mystification. Thanks to these quotations and to the journey through the Valois which they accompany, the historical past that the bibliophilic narrator sets out to find is transmuted into a foray into the intimacy of his personal past.

45. *Histoire de ma vie*, pt. 2, chap. 11, in George Sand, *Oeuvres autobiographiques*, ed. Georges Lubin (Paris: Gallimard, Bibliothèque de la Pléiade, 1970), 1:537.

46. Gregory Nagy, *Pindar's Homer: The Lyric Possession of an Epic Past* (Baltimore: Johns Hopkins University Press, 1990).

47. In his *Vie de saint Faron*, written in 869, Hildegaire cites the beginning and end of a song in honor of the saint (counselor to Dagobert and Bishop of Meaux, d. 668), which the people supposedly sang while women danced and clapped their hands. That cantilena, we are told, is reproduced in the form of a "rustic song" (*carmine rustico*). The episode for which the cantilena praises Saint Faron could not have occurred as it is related. We thus agree with Paul Zumthor—who wishes to illustrate the notion of "swerve" in that way—that this text, precisely because it is a fake, "gives us Hildegaire's notion of a certain poetry of popular usage." Zumthor, *Langue et technique poétiques à l'époque romane (XIᵉ–XIIIᵉ siè-*

cles), (Paris: Klincksieck, 1963), 51. On the cantilena of Faron, which has elicited an extremely vast body of literature, see in the last instance the excellent analyses of Michel Banniard, *Viva voice: Communication écrite et communication orale du IVᵉ au IXᵉ siècle en Occident latin* (Paris: Etudes Augustiniennes, 1992), 295–99.

48. Prologue to Marie de France, *Lais*, lines 9–42, ed. Karl Warnke, trans. Laurence Harf-Lancner (Paris: Le Livre de Poche, "Lettres Gothiques," 1990), 22–25.

49. In *Le lai du Chèvrefeuille* (262–69), Tristram signals his presence to Isolde by placing on the path she will have to take a stick from a hazelnut tree, around which a branch of honeysuckle has wound itself. Marie tells us that he engraved his name on the stick. Then, eighteen lines provide "the message of the writing that he had sent to her." These lines make explicit the symbolism of the hazelnut stick surrounded by honeysuckle: Together, they can live, but if anyone separates them, they both die. The conclusion of this development is: "Sweet love, so it is with us: you cannot live without me, nor I without you." *The Lais of Marie de France*, trans. Robert Hanning and Joan Ferrante (New York: E. P. Dutton, 1978), 191, 192. Medievalists have endlessly debated and continue to debate whether the stick bore only Tristram's name, or these two lines as well, or even, unrealistically, the totality of the message. The text is written in such a way as to make it impossible to decide. It is understood that, for me, the solution to the problem is that the problem must necessarily remain without solution.

50. Hobsbawn and Tangen, cited in Philippe Laburthe-Tolra and Jean-Pierre Warnier, *Ethnologie et anthropologie* (Paris: PUF, 1993), 9.

51. Henri Pourrat, introduction to "Chasse d'été," in *Contes de la bûcheronne* (Paris: Alsatia, 1950), 13.

52. Nicole Belmont, "Le folklore refoulé ou les déductions de l'archaïsme," in *L'homme. Anthropologie: Etat des lieux* (Paris: Le Livre de Poche, 1986), 293.

53. See Claude Lévi-Strauss, *La pensée sauvage* (Paris: Plon, 1962), 35.

54. Ibid., chap. 1, "La science du concret."

55. See Claude Lévi-Strauss, conclusion of *Structures élémentaires de la parenté*, rev. ed. (The Hague: Mouton, 1967).

56. Jean-Baptiste Vico, *Principes de la philosophie de l'histoire*, translated from *Scienza Nuova*, and preceded by a discourse on the system and life of the author by Jules Michelet (Paris: Armand Colin, Biblio-

thèque de Cluny, 1963), bk. 1, chap. 2, axiom 52. In reality, I am citing this axiom from the translation of Jules Chaix-Ruy, which is slightly different from that of Michelet (*J.-B. Vico et les âges de l'humanité* [Paris: Seghers, 1976], 134) [my translation from the French—*Trans.*].

57. Jean Leclercq, *L'amour des lettres et le désir de Dieu: Initiation aux auteurs monastiques du Moyen Age* (Paris, 1957).

58. The discoverers were Tony Hunt and Ian Short. The passage is that of the wedding night of Isolde and King Mark.

59. Yves Bonnefoy, *Les lampes*, in *Hier régnant désert* (Paris: Mercure de France, 1958). This poem, modified, became *Veneranda* in later editions (Mercure de France, 1978; Poésie/Gallimard, 1982).

Are the Songs of the Middle Ages Old Songs?

Preliminaries

1. On these two points, see Paul Zumthor, *La lettre et la voix: De la "littérature" médiévale* (Paris: Le Seuil, 1987).

2. Friedrich Nietzsche, *Untimely Meditations*, trans. R. J. Hollingdale (New York: Cambridge University Press, 1983), and idem, *On the Genealogy of Morals*, trans. Walter Kaufmann (New York: Vintage, 1969), first and second essays.

3. Georg Wilhelm Friedrich Hegel, *The Philosophy of History*, trans. J. Sibree (New York: Dover, 1956), 79.

4. Cf. John E. Jackson, *Mémoire et création* (Paris: Mercure de France, 1992).

5. Erwin Panofsky, *Perspective as Symbolic Form*, trans. Christopher S. Wood (New York: Zone, 1991), and idem, *Gothic Architecture and Scholasticism* (New York: Meridian, 1957).

6. See Bernard Guenée, *Histoire et culture historique dans l'Occident médiéval* (Paris: Aubier, 1980); Michel-Marie Dufeil, *Saint Thomas et l'histoire*, *Senefiance* 29 (1991). On the taste for history and the absence of historical consciousness in Antiquity, see Ernst Robert Curtius, *European Literature and the Latin Middle Ages*, trans. Willard R. Trask (New York: Pantheon, 1953).

"The Fairy of Legend, Eternally Young":
Popular Songs, Old Songs

1. Michel de Montaigne, *The Complete Works of Montaigne*, trans. Donald M. Frame (Stanford: Stanford University Press, 1957), 227.

2. La Villemarqué, *Barzaz-Breiz*, xxxv. See Bizet, *La poésie populaire en Allemagne*, 12–13; Miodrag Ibrovac, *Claude Fauriel et la fortune des poésies populaires grecque et serbe* (Paris: Didier, 1966), 19; and Paul Béni-chou, *Nerval et la chanson folklorique* (Paris: Corti, 1970), 34.

3. "Die Volkspoesie, ganz Natur wie sie ist, hat Naivetäten und Reize, durch die sie sich der Hauptschönheit der künstlichvolkommensten Poesie gleichet." Herder translating Montaigne in *Volkslieder, Erster Teil*, in *Werke*, 3:71.

4. "Genie est eine Sammlung Naturkräfte: es kommt also auch aus den Händen der Natur und muss vorausgehen, ehe Geschmack werden kann": These are the first words of the essay. Herder, *Ursachen des gesunkenen Geschmacks*, in *Werke* 4:113.

5. See Paul Zumthor, *Langue, texte, énigme* (Paris: Le Seuil, 1975); and idem, *Le masque et la lumière: La poétique des grands rhétoriqueurs* (Paris: Le Seuil, 1978).

6. Montaigne, *Complete Works*, 225.

7. Ibid., 226.

8. Ibid., 227.

9. Frédéric Godefroy, *Dictionnaire de l'ancienne langue française* (Paris, 1902), 10:858.

10. Montaigne, *Complete Works*, 158.

11. Montaigne, "Of Cannibals," in *Complete Works*, 152.

12. Miodrag Ibrovac asserts as a well-known fact, but without citing his sources, that the song was written by Antoine de Navarre, duke of Vendôme, and that King Henry is Henry II—which would make it a song that is not at all popular. See Ibrovac, *Claude Fauriel et la fortune*, 20.

13. Marot, *Les épigrammes: Troisiesme Livre*, in *Oeuvres poétiques*, 2:315–16. The poem was written after 1538 and probably before 1540, the date of Anne d'Alençon's marriage.

14. The letter *N* was pronounced like the name "Anne."

15. Clément Marot, song 18, in *Oeuvres poétiques*, 1:189. The song was written before 1529.

16. Cited by C. A. Mayer, in Clément Marot, *Oeuvres complètes*, vol. 3, *Oeuvres lyriques* (London: Athlone Press, 1964), 190.

17. Gérard de Nerval, *Oeuvres complètes*, ed. J. Guillaume and Claude Pichois (Paris: Pléiade, 1993), 3:550.

18. Ibid., 551.

19. Ibid., 569.

20. Ibid., 541.

21. Bénichou, *Nerval et la chanson folklorique*.

22. Nerval, *Oeuvres complètes*, 1:754.

23. See Conrad Laforte, *Survivances médiévales dans la chanson folklorique: Poétique de la chanson en laisse* (Quebec: Presses de l'Université Laval, 1981), 13, 15.

24. Nerval, *Oeuvres complètes*, 3:493.

25. Ibid., 489.

26. Ibid., 569.

27. Ibid., 573.

28. Ibid., 571.

29. Ibid., 560.

30. Ibid., 562.

31. See the excellent analyses in Jackson, *Mémoire et création poétique*, 76–91.

32. Cited in Bizet, *La poésie populaire en Allemagne*, 25.

Popular Songs and Medieval Songs

1. Bénichou, *Nerval et la chanson folklorique*, 170.

2. Paulin Paris, *Discours d'ouverture, 1ᵉʳ mars 1853, Collège de France: Cours de langue et littérature française au Moyen Age* (Paris: Collège de France, 1853), 4.

3. *Bulletin du Comité de la langue, de l'histoire et des arts de la France* (Paris, 1854), 217, cited in Bénichou, *Nerval et la chanson folklorique*, 171.

4. Parallel to the survey on popular poems, another initiative by Fortoul had the aim of publishing a "collection of ancient French poets." It was to be more successful, since in 1870 ten volumes appeared under the title *Les anciens poètes de France*.

5. *Bulletin du Comité de la langue*, 218–19.

6. Ibid., 225.

7. Bénichou, *Nerval et la chanson folklorique*, 330–31.

8. That combination of two medieval romances, *La Châtelaine de Vergy* and *Roman du châtelain de Coucy et de la dame de Fayel* by

Jakennes, was borrowed from Marguerite de Lusan's *Anecdotes de la cour de Philippe Auguste* (1733).

9. Translated and cited, indignantly, by Jean-Baptiste Weckerlin in *La chanson populaire* (Paris: Firmin-Didot, 1887), preface, ii. Unfortunately, I have not been able to get hold of Wolff's book itself.

10. Ernest Tonnelat, *Les contes des frères Grimm* (Paris, 1912).

11. Peter Burke, *Popular Culture in Early Modern Europe* (New York: New York University Press, 1978; Hants, England: Scolar Press, 1988), 5.

12. The offhandedness of that cavalier view should not lead us to think that the taste for the Middle Ages was deserting England. On the contrary, it was very keen throughout the nineteenth century: not only in the first half (is there any need to recall the success and influence of Walter Scott?) but also during the Victorian age. It was no doubt more alive in England than anywhere else in Europe and manifested itself in architecture and painting as well as literature.

13. Bizet, *La poésie populaire en Allemagne*, 15–16.

14. Ibrovac, *Claude Fauriel et la fortune*, 25.

15. This Anglo-Norman poem, written by Robert Biket at the end of the twelfth century, exploits the motif of the ordeal of chastity, which was common in Arthurian literature. A messenger brings an enchanted horn—that is, a drinking horn—to the court of King Arthur. No one can drink from it without spilling the liquid on himself if he is jealous or his wife is unfaithful. The ordeal turns to the confusion of all, beginning with King Arthur. Only Garadu or Caradoc is successful. *The Anglo-Norman Text of Le Lai du Cor*, ed. C. T. Erickson (Oxford: Anglo-Norman Text Society, 1973).

16. Literally, *volkstümlich* means "in the popular manner." In reality, however, in most cases the word is used in the sense of "popular."

17. Weckerlin, *La chanson populaire*, preface, xxix.

18. Franz Böhme, *Altdeutsches Liederbuch* (Leipzig: Breitkopf and Hpartel, 1877), cited by Weckerlin, *La chanson populaire*, preface, v–vi.

19. Note that of these two poems, the one that became a popular song was not Brentano's, which has the proper form (a narrative ballad in a stiff style, composed in distiches with long lines, a strong caesura, and two accented syllables per hemistich) but Heine's, which is in quatrains of alternating rhyme and in which the sensibility of the romantic poet is given free rein.

20. Patrice Coirault, *Formation de nos chansons folkloriques*, 4 vols. (Paris: Editions du Scarabée, 1953–63).

21. Friedrich Diez, *Altromanische Sprachdenkmale* (Bonn, 1846).

22. Alfred Jeanroy, *Les origines de la poésie lyrique en France au Moyen Age* (Paris: Champion, 1889).

23. See Ibrovac, *Claude Fauriel et la fortune*, 43–68.

24. Claude Fauriel, *Histoire de la poésie provençale* (Paris, 1847), 1:14–16.

25. Ibid., chap. 18, "Poésie des troubadours. III.-Genre populaire," 2:77–109.

26. Ibid., 94.

27. "Alle älteste Dichtung einer Nation ist volkstümlich; erst viel später tritt die Kunstdichtung auf." Julius Sahr, *Das deutsche Volkslied* (Liepzig: Sammlung Göschen, 1901), 7.

28. See Olender, *Les langues du paradis*.

29. "Die Romanischen Sprachen, wie sie aus den Trümmern der Roemischen hervorgewachsen, sind sie besonders ein überzeugendes Beweis der Analogie die zwischen dem Wirken der Natur und dem Menschengeist besteht, der Gleichmaessigkeit mit welcher in beiden Gott waltet und sich offenbart. . . . Zugleich aber, da die Romanischen Sprachen mehr dem Bewusstsein und der Willkür der Menschen anheimgestellt waren, welche Menschen-Aermlichkeit und Unbehilflichkeit hier gegen die Kraft, den Reichtum, die Geschmeidigkeit der Germanischen und aller jener Sprachen, an deren Schöpfung der Mensch keinen Teil hat, deren Ursprung ein wunderbares Geheimnis bedeckt, deren Worte zugleich mit den Dingen welche sie benennen erschaffen sind." Wilhelm Wackernagel, *Altfranzösische Lieder und Leiche aus Handschriften zu Berne und Neuenburg* (Basel, 1846), intro., iv–v.

30. P. Coirault, *Notre chanson folklorique (Etude d'information générale): L'objet et la méthode. L'inculte et son apport. L'élaboration. La notion* (Paris: Picard, 1942), 54–55.

31. Herder, *Stimmen der Völker in Liedern*, 7; cited and translated in Weckerlin, *La chanson populaire*, 1; this quotation opens chapter 1.

32. Bibliothèque de l'Institut de France, Fauriel collection 2348 (1–2), course on the chivalric romances, second year, folio 274. The course dealt with Guillaume d'Orange, Jaufré, and Perceval.

33. La Villemarqué, *Barzaz-Breiz*.

34. Francis Gourvil, *Théodore-Claude-Henri Hersart de La Villemarqué (1815–1895) et le "Barzaz-Breiz" (1839, 1845, 1867)* (Rennes: Imprimerie Oberthur, 1960).

35. Donatien Laurent, *Aux sources du Barzaz-Breiz: La mémoire d'un*

peuple (Douarnenez: Ar Men, 1989). See Bernadette Bricout, *Contes et récits du Livradois: Textes recueillis par Henri Pourrat* (Paris: Maisonneuve et Larose, 1989), and *Le savoir et la saveur: Henri Pourrat et Le trésor des contes* (Paris: Gallimard, 1992).

36. Ermoldus Nigelus, *Poème sur Louis le Pieux et Epitres au roi Pépin*, ed. and trans. Edmond Faral (Paris: Les Belles Lettres, 1932), 98–132.

37. *The Second Continuation*, lines 23598–703.

38. La Villemarqué, *Barzaz-Breiz*, 151.

39. Ibid., 151–52. My ignorance of Breton obliges me to cite only La Villemarqué's translation [my translation from the French—*Trans.*].

40. Ibid., 154.

41. Marie de France, *Lais*, 216–17, lines 126–29; *The Lais of Marie de France*, 158.

42. [Harf-Lancner, whose modern French translation Zink cites above, translates the last line as "et continuer à voir mon ami."—*Trans.*]

43. La Villemarqué, *Barzaz-Breiz*, 81.

44. Chrétien de Troyes, *Romans*, 950, lines 267–26; Chrétien de Troyes, *Perceval: The Story of the Grail*, trans. Nigel Bryant (Totowa, N.J.: Rowman and Littlefield, 1982), 4.

45. Chrétien de Troyes, *Romans*, 946–47, lines 131–43; idem, *Perceval*, 2.

46. Chrétien de Troyes, *Romans*, 948, lines 168–73; idem, *Perceval*, 3.

47. François Villon, *Poésies complètes*, ed. Claude Thiry (Paris: Le Livre de Poche, "Lettres Gothiques," 1991), 163, lines 892–98; idem, "His Mother's Service to Our Lady," trans. Dante Gabriel Rossetti, in *The Ballads and Lyrics of François Villon* (Mount Vernon, N.Y.: Peter Pauper, 1940), 58.

48. La Villemarqué, *Barzaz-Breiz*, 107–8.

49. Ibid., 110.

50. *Le Moniteur*, 22 May 1845, cited by La Villemarqué, *Barzaz-Breiz*, lxxvi.

The Temptation of a Prehistory

1. M. P. G. de Chabanon, *De la musique considérée en elle-même et dans ses rapports avec la parole, les langues, la poésie et le théâtre* (Paris: Pissot, 1785), 3; cited in Claude Lévi-Strauss, *Regarder, écouter, lire* (Paris: Plon, 1993), 113.

2. Pascal Quignard, *La leçon de musique* (Paris: Hachette, 1987), 27.

3. Julien Tiersot, *Histoire de la chanson populaire en France* (Paris: E. Plon, 1889), 536. These are the last words of the book.

4. Weckerlin, *La chanson populaire*, 6, and M. Tresch, *Evolution de la chanson française savante et populaire* (Luxemburg, 1921), 14–15.

5. Paul Verrier, *Le vers français: Formes primitives—Développement—Diffusion*, 3 vols. (Paris, Didier, 1931–32).

6. Conrad Laforte, *Le catalogue de la chanson folklorique française*, vol. 1, *Chansons en laisse* (Quebec: Presses de l'Université Laval, 1977), and *Survivances médiévales dans la chanson folklorique*. See also his *La chanson folklorique et les ecrivains du XIXᵉ siècle (en France et au Québec* (Montreal: Editions Hurtubise HMH, 1973).

7. Jeanroy, *Les origines de la poésie lyrique*, 1–2.

8. "Dass ich die altfranzösischen Romanzen und Pastourellen zusammen gefasst habe, ist nicht zufällig, sondern mit gutem Bedacht geschehen. Beide ruhen auf volksthümlicher Grundlage und haben volksthümliche Elemente in sich aufgenommen. Bei dem bedauerlichen Verluste, der die romanische Volkslyrik des Mittelalters betroffen hat, sind sie daher hohem Werte; sie bilden die hervorragendsten und bedeutendsten Gattungen der nordfranzösischen Lyrik, neben denen die übrigen farblos erscheinen und von der reicheren südfranzösischen überstrahlt werden." Karl Bartsch, ed., *Altfranzösische Romanzen und Pastourellen* (Leipzig, 1870), v.

9. See Jeanroy, *Les origines de la poésie lyrique*, xviii ff.

10. See, among others, Pierre Bec, *La lyrique française au Moyen Age (XIIᵉ–XIIIᵉ siècles): Contribution à une typologie des genres poétiques médiévaux* (Paris: A. and J. Picard): vol. 1, *Etudes* (1977); vol. 2, *Textes* (1978); Ulrich Mölk, *Romanische Frauenlieder* (Munich: Wilhelm Fink, 1989); Pilar Lorenzo Gradin, *La cancion de mujer en la lirica medieval* (Santiago de Compostela: Universidade de Santiago de Compostela, 1990).

11. Edmond Faral, "La pastourelle," *Romania* 49 (1923): 204–59; Maurice Delbouille, "Les origines de la pastourelle," Mémoires de l'Académie Royale de Belgique, Classe des lettres et des sciences morales et politiques, Deuxième série, tome 20, 1927. See Michel Zink, *La pastourelle: Poésie et folklore au Moyen Age* (Paris: Bordas, 1972).

Edmond Faral, "Les chansons de toile ou chansons d'histoire," *Romania* 69 (1946–47): 433–62. See Zink, *Les chansons de toile*.

12. Elvira Gangutia Elicegui, "Poesia grieza 'de amigo' y poesia arabizoespañola," *Emerita: Revista de Linguistica y Filologia Clasica* 40 (1972): 329–96.

13. Michel Zink, "Lubias et Bélissant dans la chanson d'*Ami et Amile*," in *Les voix de la conscience* (Caen: Paradigme, 1992), 101–14.

14. Zink, *Les chansons de toile*, 82–84.

15. Paris, *Chansons du XVᵉ siècle*, 32–33.

16. Jeanroy, *Les origines de la poésie lyrique*; Gaston Paris, "Les origines de la poésie lyrique en France au Moyen Age" (review of Jeanroy's thesis), *Journal des Savants* (1891): 674–88, 729–42; (1892): 155–67, 407–29; article reprinted in *Mélanges de Littérature Française du Moyen Age*, ed. Mario Roques (Paris: Champion, 1912), 539–615; Joseph Bédier, "Les fêtes de mai," *Revue des Deux Mondes*, 1 May 1896, 146–72.

17. Karl Bartsch, *Chrestomathie provençale (Xᵉ–XVᵉ siècles)*, entirely rewritten by Eduard Koschwitz (Marburg: M. G. Elwert, 1904), 121–22.

18. Bartsch, *Altfranzösische Romanzen und Pastourellen*, 23–24.

19. See Zink, *La pastourelle*, and idem, "La suffisance du paysan dans la littérature française du Moyen Age," in *Der Bauer im Wandel der Zeit*, ed. Willi Hirdt (Bonn: Bouvier Verlag, 1986), 35–48; reprinted in *Les voix de la conscience*, 247–60.

20. See Zink, *Les chansons de toile*, 51–60.

21. See Jeanroy, *Les origines de la poésie lyrique*, 363–86.

22. "A man vouches for the virtue of a woman against another man, who undertakes to seduce her; as a result of deceptive appearances, the woman seems in fact to have given in to the seducer, but her innocence is finally acknowledged." Gaston Paris, "Le cycle de la gageure," *Romania* 32 (1903): 481. This extremely widespread tale provided the Middle Ages with the subject of anecdotes, short stories, and numerous romances. Gaston Paris gives an accounting of them; they include *Le roman du comte de Poitiers*, *Guillaume de Dole*, and Gerbert de Montreuil's *Roman de la Violette*, which was inspired by the first two. In the modern era, Musset's *La quenouille de Barberine* exploits a similar theme. Jean Renart omits the slightly shocking element of the bet, which makes his romance a kind of wager tale without the wager. See Michel Zink, *Roman rose et rose rouge: Le Roman de la Rose ou de Guillaume de Dole de Jean Renart* (Paris: Nizet, 1979), 45–68.

23. Zink, *Roman rouge et rose rouge*, and idem, *Les chansons de toile*, 3–12.

24. In Zink, *Les chansons de toile*, 161–64; Renart, *Romance of the Rose or Guillaume de Dole*, 49–50.

25. Adam de la Halle, *Oeuvres complètes*, ed. and trans. Pierre-Yves

Badel (Paris: Le Livre de Poche, "Lettres Gothiques," 1995), 368–69, lines 1017–27. Cf. Zink, *Les chansons de toile*, 18.

26. Renart, *Le roman de la rose ou de Guillaume de Dole*, lines 22235–94.

27. Zumthor, *Essai de poétique médiévale*, 290–98.

28. *Guillaume de Dole* is dated 1210 by some (R. Lejeune, J. Baldwin), 1228 by others (F. Lecoy). The other narrative texts into which *chansons de toile* are inserted are more recent. Paris manuscript BNF fr. 20050 (*chansonnier* of Saint-Germain-des-Prés), which contains a series of them, dates from the middle of the thirteenth century.

29. Gerbert de Montreuil, *Le roman de Violette ou de Gérard de Nevers*, ed. Douglas Labarce Buffum (Paris: SATF, 1928); Henri d'Andeli, *Le lai d'Aristote*, ed. Maurice Delbrouille (Paris: Les Belles Lettres, 1951).

30. Champfleury, *Lettre à M. Ampère* (1853), cited in Bénichou, *Nerval et la chanson folklorique*, 348.

31. *Chansons de toile. XIIᵉ siècle. Edition en vieux français*, trans. Henry Poulaille and Régine Pernoud, illus. Joëlle Desternes (Paris: Jacques Rogers, distributed by Max P. Delatte, 1947).

The Fresh Source of Songs

1. See Nico H. J. Van Den Boogaard, *Rondeaux et refrains du XIIᵉ au début du XIVᵉ siècle* (Paris: Klincksieck, 1969).

2. Hans Spanke, *G. Raynauds Bibliographie des altfranzösichen Liedes* (Leiden, 1955), no. 1698 I and II; Bartsch, *Altfranzösische Romanzen und Pastourellen*, 1:49, 50–51; Van den Boogaard, *Rondeaux et refrains*, nos. 1396 and 1348.

3. Rondeau inserted into Jean Renart, *Le roman de la Rose ou de Guillaume de Dole*, line 1579; idem, *The Romance of the Rose or Guillaume de Dole*, 40 [translation modified]. Van den Boogaard, *Rondeaux et refrains*, 9:29. On the rondeau of the lovely Aélis and *Guillaume de Dole*, see Carlos Alvar, "Algunos aspectos de la lirica medieval: El caso de Belle Aeliz," in *Symposium in honorem prof. Martin de Riquer* (Barcelona: Quaderno Crema, 1986), 21–49.

4. See Michel Zink, "Le lyrisme en rond: Esthétique et séductions des poèmes à forme fixe au Moyen Age," *Cahiers de l'Association Internationale des Etudes Françaises* 32 (1980): 71–90; reprinted in *Les voix de la conscience*, 177–96.

5. See Alvar, "Algunos aspectos." Baude de la Quarière's potpourri is reproduced from *La chanson de Bele Aelis, par le trouvère Baude de la Quarière*, metrical study by R. Meyer, interpretive essay by J. Bédier, musical study by P. Aubry (Paris: A. Picard, 1904), 47–49.

6. See, for example, M.-D. Chenu, "Notes de lexicographie philosophique médiévale: *Antiqui, moderni*," *Revue des Sciences Philosophiques et Théologiques* 17 (1928): 82–94; Bernard Guenée, "Temps de l'histoire et temps de la mémoire au Moyen Age," *Annuaire-Bulletin de la Société de l'Histoire de la France* (1976–77):23–25; idem, *Histoire et culture historique dans l'Occident médiéval* (Paris: Aubier, 1980); Michel-Marie Dufeil, *"De antiquitate secundum Tomam"*, Weiner Arbeiten zur germanischen Altertumskunde und Philologie, 1981, reprinted in *Saint Thomas et l'histoire* (Aix-en-Provence: Université de Provence, 1991), 42–63.

7. Curtius, *European Literature and the Latin Middle Ages.*

8. See Michel Zink, *La subjectivité littéraire: Autour du siècle de saint Louis* (Paris: PUF, 1985), 47–74.

9. Nicolò Pasero, ed., *Guglielmo IX: Poesie* (Modena: S.T.E.M., 1973), 297.

10. Guillaume de Machaut, *Dit de la Fleur de Lis et de la Marguerité*, ed. Anthime Fourrier; and Jean Froissart, *"Dits" et "Débats" avec en appendice quelques poèmes de Guillaume de Machaut*, ed. Anthime Fourrier (Geneva: Droz, 1979),295, lines 207–12.

11. Marie de France, *Lanval*, in *Lais*, 138–39, lines 94–96; *Lais of Marie de France*, 107 [translation slightly modified].

12. Bartsch, *Altfranzösische Romanzen und Pastourellen*, bk. 2, vol. 2:104, lines 25–30.

13. Marcabru, song 32, in *Poésies complètes du troubadour Marcabru*, ed. J.-M.-L. Dejeanne (Toulouse: E. Privat, 1909), 152, lines 1–2. The word *vers* has a meaning more precise than "poem." Among the first troubadours, it designated the type of piece their successors would call *canso* (song).

14. Jean Boutière and A.-H. Schutz, *Biographies des troubadours: Textes provençaux des XIIIe et XIVe siècles*, rewritten ed. (Paris: Nizet, 1964), 9.

15. Renart, *Le roman de la Rose ou de Guillaume de Dole*, lines 1148–51.

16. See Antoine Tavera, "Les chants du crépuscule à l'aube du *trobar*," in *Fin des temps et temps de la fin dans l'univers médiéval* (Aix-en-Provence: Université de Provence, 1993), 495–517.

17. Boutière and Schutz, *Biographies des troubadours*, 14.

18. On this point and on the implications of the rejection of the springtime stanza, judged outdated and incompatible with the requirements of *fin'amor*, see Zink, *La subjectivité littéraire*, 52–55.

19. Alfred Jeanroy, ed., *Jongleurs et troubadours gascons des XIIe et XIIIe siècles* (Paris: Champion, CFMA, 1939; reprint, 1957), iv.

20. Ms. Paris Bibl. Nat. Fr. fr. 12744, in Paris, *Chansons du XVe siècle*; Ms. Paris Bibl. Nat. Fr. fr. 9346 (Bayeux manuscript), in Gérold, *Le manuscrit de Bayeux*. These songs are also available in the newly edited volume *Chansons des XVe et XVIe siècles*, texts presented by Françoise Ferrand (Paris: UGE 10/18, Bibliothèque Médiévale, 1986).

21. On the implications, ambiguities, and inadequacies of the very expression "popular song," to which he prefers "folkloric song," which has generally been adopted by his successors, see Coirault, *Notre chanson folklorique*, 54–55. As often, Coirault's analysis is at once vehement, penetrating, and confused.

22. Laforte, *Le catalogue de la chanson folklorique française*, and idem, *Survivances médiévales dans la chanson folklorique*. What Laforte calls the "song in laisses" is the song made up of long homophonic lines with a strong caesura, which is so common in the French repertoire. That very expression, as indicated by the title of the second work cited, emphasizes the continuity of medieval lyricism and the folkloric song in a manner that neither Herder nor La Villemarqué would have disavowed.

23. Gérold, *Le manuscrit de Bayeux*, 16. On the court songs of the fifteenth century, see the recent work by Kemp, *Burgundian Court Song in the Time of Binchois*.

24. Gérold, *Le manuscrit de Bayeux*, xxxvii–xxxviii.

25. Paris, *Chansons du XVe siècle*, v–vi.

26. "This song, so popular in tone and manner, displays incoherencies that are perhaps original and that in any case are impossible to set aside." Ibid., 115.

27. Gérold, *Le manuscrit de Bayeux*, viii.

28. Ibid.

29. Ibid., xxviii–xxix.

30. Rudolf Adelbert Meyer, *Französische Lieder aus der Florentiner Handschrift Strozzi-Magliabecchiana CL. VII. 1040*, Beihefte zur Zeitschrift für romanische Philologie 7 (Halle: Niemeyer, 1907).

31. Henri Davenson, *Le livre des chansons* (Neuchâtel: La Baconnière, 1946), 16.

32. Gaston Paris, "De l'étude de la poésie populaire en France," *Mélusine* 1 (1878): 1–6; excerpted from *Revue Critique*, 22 May 1866; Jules Gilliéron, "*La Claire Fontaine*, chanson populaire française: Examen critique des diverses versions," *Romania* 12 (1883): 307–31.

33. "That poetry has remained the basis and model for the popular poetry that followed and for that which is still being produced. In a remarkable reaction, it emerged during the era when literature properly speaking was the farthest from nature, from simplicity, and from true feeling. In the fifteenth century, which opened with Alain Chartier and ended with Crétin, when *the art and science of rhetoric* flourished, when tiresome allegory and the ungainly imitation of Latin reigned without rival, when only Villon . . . made the muse descend from her solemn pedestal and led her, not into the fields, but into the muddy streets of Paris—an entirely new vein of poetry, plentiful, fresh, and delectable, came to well up in a few provinces and to quietly begin to babble. That is the true French current, which leaks out through a fissure, instead of being forced into those pompous machines that produce fountains of water and waterfalls to delight the eyes of princes. The poetic *waterworks* of that time have long since gone dry . . . ; but the thin stream of water that escaped during the time of Joan of Arc is still running, and we still take pleasure in drinking from the palm of our hand a few drops of that limpid water, which shimmers gaily in the sun among the grasses and gravel." Paris, *Chansons du XVᵉ siècle*, ix.

34. Je dis le loup, car tous les loups
Ne sont pas de la même sorte;
Il en est d'une humeur accorte,
Sans bruit, sans fiel et sans courroux,
Qui privés, complaisants et doux,
Suivent les jeunes Demoiselles
Jusque dans les maisons, jusque dans les ruelles;
Mais hélas! Qui ne sait pas que ces Loups doucereux,
De tous les Loups sont les plus dangereux.

I say the wolf, for all wolves
Are not of the same kind;
There are some of a pleasing manner,
Noiseless, without malice or ire,
Who, private, obliging, and sweet,
Follow young maidens

Even into their houses, even into their rooms;
But alas! Who does not know that these smooth-talking Wolves
Are of all Wolves the most dangerous?

35. Bayeux 85. We follow the edition of Françoise Ferrand, *Chansons des XVᵉ et XVIᵉ siècles*, 155. [*Dondaine* is a kind of bagpipe. *Donde, ho, hu, hayne*, etc., are all more or less nonsense syllables—*Trans.*]

36. See Michel Rousse, "Les chansons dans les farces," in *Musique, littérature et société*, Actes du colloque d'Amiens, ed. Danielle Buschinger (Paris: Champion, 1980), 451 ff.

37. "Planctum beate Agnetis in sonu, El bosc d'Argena justal palaih, Amfos, A la fenestra de la plus auta tor." *Le jeu de sainte Agnès: Drame provençal du XIVᵉ siècle*, ed. Alfred Jeanroy, with transcription of the melodies by T. Gérold (Paris: Champion, CFMA, 1931).

38. Sand, *Histoire de ma vie*, pt. 2, chap. 11, 1:537.

39. Nous n'irons plus au bois, les lauriers sont coupés.
Les Amours des bassins, les Naïades en groupe
Voient reluire au soleil en cristaux découpés
Les flots silencieux qui coulaient de leur coupe.
Les lauriers sont coupés, et le cerf aux abois
Tressaille au son du cor; nous n'irons plus au bois,
Où des enfants joueurs riait la folle troupe
Parmis les lys d'argent aux pleurs du ciel trempés,
Voici l'herbe qu'on fauche et les lauriers qu'on coupe.
Nous n'irons plus aux bois, les lauriers sont coupés.

We shall go no more to the woods, the laurels trees are
    cut down.
The fountain Cupids, the Naiads in a group
See shining in the sun in jagged crystals
The silent streams that poured from their cup.
The laurel trees are cut down, and the stag at bay
Shudders at the sound of the horn; we shall go no more
    to the woods,
Where at playing children the mad company laughed
Among the silver lilies, drenched in the tears of the sky,
Here is the grass they mow down and the laurels they cut.
We shall go no more to the woods, the laurel trees are
    cut down.

Théodore de Banville, *Stalactites* (Paris, 1846), 7, cited in Bénichou, *Nerval et la chanson folklorique*, 354.

40. "And then, when we succeeded in discovering one of these nests where songs are still sung, how many precautions did we not have to take so as not to frighten off the singers, who at first declared they no longer remembered anything, that they had forgotten everything, or nearly." And Weckerlin adds: "Once begun, for example, they sing to you, they rattle on and on at you, to the point that you no longer know how to stop them. . . . That was how it was in our youth, now gone by. Today, what a change! Thanks to the ease in communication, where are those wild and primitive regions that kept their old language and the tradition of their fathers' mores?" Hence, in the end, the author turns to his own account the impression of his informers. Weckerlin, *La chanson populaire*, xxx–xxxi.

Bibliography

The list of books and articles cited and used in this book is, like it, eclectic and dispersed. It is in no way a systematic bibliography.

Adam de la Halle. *Oeuvres complètes*. Edited and translated by Pierre-Yves Badel. Paris: Le Livre de Poche, "Lettres Gothiques," 1995.

Alvar, Carlos. "Algunos aspectos de la lírica medieval: El caso de Belle Aeliz." In *Symposium in honorem prof. Martin de Riquer*, 21–49. Barcelona: Quaderno Crema, 1986.

Apollinaire, Guillaume. *Alcools*. Paris: Mercure de France, 1913.

Baculard d'Arnaud, François de. *Les épreuves du sentiment*. Paris: Le Jay, 1772.

Bähler, Ursula. "Notes sur l'acception du terme de philologie romane chez Gaston Paris." *Vox Romanica* 54 (1995): 23–40.

Ballard, Christophe. *Airs nouveaux, sérieux; gaillards, à boire et des opéras comme aussi sur divers autres sujets*. 6 vols. Paris, 1698–1700.

———. *Rondes à danser*. Paris, 1724.

Banniard, Michel. *Viva voce: Communication écrite et communication orale du IVe au IXe siècle en Occident latin*. Paris: Etudes Augustiniennes, 1992.

Banville, Théodore de. *Stalactites*. Paris, 1846.

Bartsch, Karl, ed. *Altfranzösische Romanzen und Pastourellen*. Leipzig, 1870.

————, ed. *Chrestomathie provençale (Xᵉ–XVᵉ siècles)*, entirely rewritten by Eduard Koschwitz. Marburg, 1904.

Bec, Pierre. *La lyrique française au Moyen Age (XIIᵉ–XIIIᵉ siècles): Contribution à une typologie des genres poétiques médiévaux.* Paris: A. and J. Picard, 1977–78. Vol. 1, *Etudes*; vol. 2, *Textes*.

Bédier, Joseph. *Les fabliaux: Etudes de littérature populaire et d'histoire littéraire du Moyen Age.* Paris: Champion, 1893.

————. "Les fêtes de mai." *Revue des Deux Mondes*, 1 May 1896, 146–72.

————. *Le Roman de Tristan et Iseut renouvelé.* Preface by Gaston Paris. Paris: H. Piazza, 1900.

————. "Les plus anciennes danses françaises." *Revue des Deux Mondes*, 15 January 1906, 398–424.

————. *Les légendes épiques.* 4 vols. Paris: Champion, 1908–13.

————. *La chanson de Roland commentée.* Paris: H. Piazza, 1927.

————. *La chanson de Roland publiée d'après le manuscrit d'Oxford et traduite.* 6th (definitive) ed. Paris: H. Piazza, 1937.

Belmont, Nicole. "Le folklore refoulé ou les déductions de l'archaïsme." In *L'homme. Anthropologie: Etat des lieux*, 287–98. Paris: Le Livre de Poche, 1986.

Bénichou, Paul. *Nerval et la chanson folklorique.* Paris: José Corti, 1970.

Bibliothèque universelle des romans. Edited by Marquis de Paulmy, Marquis de Bastide, and Count de Tressan. 23 vols. 1775–89. Reprint, Geneva: Slatkine, 1969.

Bizet, J.-A. *La poésie populaire en Allemagne: Etude suivie d'un choix de "Volkslieder" avec traduction et notes.* Paris: Aubier, 1959.

Bloch, R. Howard, and Stephen G. Nichols, eds. *Medievalism and the Modernist Temper.* Baltimore: Johns Hopkins University Press, 1995.

Böhme, Franz. *Altdeutsches Liederbuch.* Leipzig, 1877.

Bonnefoy, Yves. *Hier régnant désert.* Paris: Mercure de France, 1958.

Boutière, Jean, and A.-H. Schutz. *Biographies des troubadours: Textes provençaux des XIIIᵉ et XIVᵉ siècles.* Rewritten ed. Paris: Nizet, 1964.

Bricout, Bernadette. *Contes et récits du Livradois: Textes recueillis par Henri Pourrat.* Paris: Maisonneuve et Larose, 1989.

————. *Le savoir et la saveur: Henri Pourrat et le Trésor des Contes.* Paris: Gallimard, 1992.

Burke, Peter. *Popular Culture in Early Modern Europe.* New York: New York University Press, 1978; Hants, England: Scholar Press, 1988.

Chabanon, M. P. G. *De la musique considérée en elle-même et dans ses rapports avec la parole, les langues, la poésie et le théâtre.* Paris: Pissot, 1785.

Chaix-Ruy. *J.-B. Vico et les âges de l'humanité*. Paris: Seghers, 1967.

La chanson de Bele Aelis, par le trouvère Baude de la Quarière. Metrical study by R. Meyer, interpretive essay by J. Bédier, musical study by P. Aubry. Paris: A. Picard, 1904.

Chanson de toile. XIIᵉ siècle. Edition en vieux français. Modern French version by Henry Poulaille and Régine Pernoud, illustrations by Joëlle Desternes. Paris: Jacques Rogers, distributed by Max P. Delatte, 1947.

Chenu, M.-D. "Notes de lexicographie philosophique médiévale: *Antiqui, moderni*." *Revue des Sciences Philosophiques et Théologiques* 17 (1928): 82–94.

Chrétien de Troyes. *Arthurian Romances*. Edited and translated by W. W. Comfort. New York: E. P. Dutton, 1935.

———. *Perceval: The Story of the Grail*. Translated by Nigel Bryant. Totowa, N.J.: Rowman and Littlefield, 1982.

———. *Romans*. Edited by Michel Zink. Paris: Le Livre de Poche, La Pochothèque, 1994.

Coirault, Patrice. *Notre chanson folklorique (Etude d'information générale). L'objet et la méthode. L'inculte et son apport. L'élaboration. La notion.* Paris: Picard, 1942.

———. *Formation de nos chansons folkloriques*. 4 vols. Paris: Editions du Scarabée, 1953–63.

Curtius, Ernst Robert. *European Literature and the Latin Middle Ages*. Translated by Willard R. Trask. New York: Pantheon, 1953.

Dakyns, J. R. *The Middle Ages in French Literatures, 1851–1900*. Oxford: Oxford University Press, 1973.

Davenson, Henri [Henri-Irénée Marrou]. *Le livre des chansons*. Neuchâtel: La Baconnière, 1946.

Delbouille, Maurice. "Les origines de la pastourelle," Mémoires de l'Académie Royale de Belgique, classe des lettres et des sciences morales et politiques. Deuxième série, tome 20, 1927.

Diez, Friedrich. *Altromanische Sprachdenkmale*. Bonn, 1846.

Doncieux, Georges. *Le Romancero populaire de la France: Choix de chansons populaires françaises*. Critical texts, with a foreword and musical index by Julien Tiersot. Paris: E. Bouillon, 1904.

Dronke, Peter. "Nuevas observaciones sobre las jaryas mozárabes." *El Crotalon: Anuario de Filologia española* 1 (1984): 99–114.

Dufeil, Michel-Marie. "*De antiquitate secundum Tomam*," Wiener Arbeiten zur germanischen Altertumskunde und Philologie, 1981. Reprinted in *Saint Thomas et l'histoire, Senefiance* 29 (1991): 42–63.

Erickson, C. T., ed. *The Anglo-Norman Text of Le Lai du Cor*. Oxford: Anglo-Norman Text Society, 1973.

Ermoldus Nigellus. *Poème sur Louis le Pieux et Epîtres au roi Pépin*. Edited and translated by Edmond Faral. Paris: Les Belles Lettres, 1932.

Faral, Edmond. "La pastourelle." *Romania* 49 (1923): 204–59.

———. "Les chansons de toile ou chansons d'histoire." *Romania* 69 (1946–47): 433–62.

Fauriel, Claude. *Histoire de la poésie provençale*. 2 vols. Paris, 1847.

Ferrand, Françoise, ed. *Chansons des XVᵉ et XVIᵉ siècles*. Paris: UGE 10/18, Bibliothèque Médiévale, 1986.

Flaubert, Gustave. *La première Education sentimentale*. Edited by Martine Bercot. Paris: Le Livre de Poche, 1993.

France, Anatole. *Abeille*. *La Revue Bleue* (1882–83).

———. *Abeille*. In *Balthusar*. Paris: Calmann-Lévy, 1889.

———. *Le crime de Sylvestre Bonnard, membre de l'Institut*. Paris: Calman-Lévy, 1881, edition reworked in 1902 and 1922.

———. *Oeuvres*. Tome 1. Edition established, presented, and annotated by Marie-Claire Bancquart. Paris: Gallimard, Bibliothèque de la Pléiade, 1984.

Froissart, Jean. *"Dits" et "Débats," avec en appendice quelques poèmes de Guillaume de Machaut*. Edited by Anthime Fourrier. Geneva: Droz, 1979.

Gangutia Elicegui, Elvira. "Poesie griega 'de amigo' y poesia arabico-española." *Emerita: Revista de Linguistica y Filologia Clasica* 40 (1972): 329–96.

———. "La poesia griega 'de amigo' y los recientes hallazgos de Arquiloco," *Emerita: Revista de Linguistica y Filologia Clasica* 45 (1977): 1–6.

Genlis, Mme de. *Les chevaliers du Cygne ou la Cour de Charlemagne, contes pour servir de suite aux "Veillées du château," et dont tous les traits qui peuvent faire allusion à la Révolution française sont tirés de l'histoire*. Paris: Lemierre, 1795.

Gennrich, Friedrich, ed. *Rondeaux, Virelais und Balladen aus dem Ende des XII., dem XIII. und dem ersten Drittel des XIV. Jahrhunderts mit des überlieferten Melodien*. 2 vols. Dresden, 1921; Göttingen, 1927.

———. *Grundriss einer Formenlehre des mittelalterlichen Liedes als Grundlage einer musikalischen Formenlehre des Liedes*. Halle: Max Niemeyer, 1932.

Gerbert de Montreuil. *Le roman de la Violette ou de Gérard de Nevers.* Edited by Douglas Labaree Buffum. Paris: SATF, 1928.

Gérold, Théodore. *Le manuscrit de Bayeux: Texte et musique d'un recueil de chansons du XVe siècle.* Strasbourg: Public. de la Faculté des Lettres, 1921.

Gilliéron, Jules. "*La Claire Fontaine,* chanson populaire française: Examen critique des diverses versions." *Romania* 12 (1883): 307–31.

Godefroy, Frédéric. *Dictionnaire de l'ancienne langue française.* Paris, 1902.

Gossman, Lionel. *Medievalism and the Ideologies of the Enlightenment: The World and Work of La Curne de Sainte-Palaye.* Baltimore: Johns Hopkins Press, 1970.

Gourvil, Francis. *Théodore-Claude-Henri Hersart de La Villemarqué (1815–1895) et le "Barzaz-Breiz" (1839, 1845, 1867).* Rennes: Imprimerie Oberthur, 1960.

Gruber, Jörn. *Die Dialektik des Trobar: Untersuchungen zur Struktur und Entwicklung des occitanischen und französischen Minnesangs des 12. Jahrhunderts.* Beihefte zur Zeitschrift für Romanische Philologie 194. Tübingen: Niemeyer, 1983.

Guenée, Bernard. "Temps de l'histoire et temps de la mémoire au Moyen Age." *Annuaire-Bulletin de la Société de l'Histoire de la France* (1976–77): 25–35.

———. *Histoire et culture historique dans l'Occident médiéval.* Paris: Aubier, 1980.

Hegel, Georg Wilhelm Friedrich. *The Philosophy of History.* Translated by J. Sibree. New York: Dover, 1956.

———. *Ästhetik.* 2 vols. Stuttgart: Phipp Reclam Jun., 1971.

Heger, Klaus. *Die bisher veröffentlichten Hargas und ihre Deutungen.* Tübingen: M. Niemeyer, 1960.

Henri d'Andeli. *Le Lai d'Aristote.* Edited by Maurice Delbouille. Paris: Les Belles Lettres, 1951.

Herder, Johann Gottfried. *Une autre philosophie de l'histoire: Auch eine Philosophie der Geschichte.* Original text and French translation by Max Rouché. Paris: Aubier, Domaine Allemand Bilingue, 1964.

———. *Sämtliche Werke.* Vol. 8. Edited by B. Suphan. Hildesheim: Olms, 1967.

———. *Idées sur la philosophie de l'histoire de l'humanité: Livres choisis.* Translated by Edgar Quinet. Introduction, notes, and dossier by Marc Crépon. Paris: Presses Pocket, 1991.

————. *Traité de l'origine des langages*. Translated by Denise Modigliani, followed by *La céleste étincelle de Prométhée, essai sur la philosophie du langage dans le discours de Herder*, by Denise Modligliani. Paris: PUF, 1992.

————. *Werke, in zehn Bänden*. Edited by Martin Bollacher, Jürgen Brummack, Christoph Bultmann, Ulrich Gaier, Gunter E. Grimm, Hans Dietrich Irmscher, Rudolf Smend, Rainer Wisbert, and Thomas Zippert. Frankfurt-am-Main: Deutscher Klassiker Verlag. Vol. 3, 1990; vol. 4, 1994.

Hersart de la Villemarqué, Théodore. *Barzaz-Breiz: Chants populaires de la Bretagne recueillis et publiés avec une traduction française, des éclairissements, des notes et les mélodies originales*. Paris, 1839. Rev. ed., 1867. Reprint, Paris: Libraire Académique Perrin, 1959; Maspéro, 1983.

Hirdt, Willi, ed. *Romanistik: Eine Bonner Erfindung*. 2 vols. Bonn: Bouvier Verlag, 1993.

Hitchcock, Richard. *The Kharjas Research, Bibliographics, and Checklists*. London: Grant and Cutler, 1977.

Ibrovac, Miodrag. *Claude Fauriel et la fortune des poésies populaires grecque et serbe*. Paris: Didier, 1966.

Jackson, John E. *Mémoire et création poétique*. Paris: Mercure de France, 1992.

Jeanroy, Alfred. *Les origines de la poésie lyrique en France au Moyen Age*. Paris: Champion, 1889.

————, ed. *Le jeu de sainte Agnès: Drame provençal du XIVᵉ siècle . . . avec la transcription des mélodies par Th. Gérold*. Paris: Champion, CFMA, 1931.

————, ed. *Jongleurs et troubadours gascons des XIIᵉ et XIIIᵉ siècles*. Paris: Champion, CFMA, 1939. Reprint, 1957.

Kemp, Walter H. *Burgundian Court Song in the Time of Binchois: The Anonymous "Chansons: of El Escorial, ms. V. III.24*. Oxford: Clarendon Press, 1990.

Laburthe-Tolra, Philippe, and Jean-Pierre Warnier. *Ethnologie et anthropologie*. Paris: PUF, 1993.

Laforte, Conrad. *La chanson folklorique et les écrivains du XIXᵉ siècle (en France et au Québec)*. Montreal: Editions Hurtubise HMH, 1973.

————. *Le catalogue de la chanson folklorique française, I: Chansons en laisse*. Quebec: Presses de l'Université Laval, 1977.

————. *Survivances médiévales dans la chanson folklorique: Poétique de la chanson en laisse*. Quebec: Presses de l'Université Laval, 1981.

Laurent, Donatien. *Aux sources du Barzaz-Breiz: La mémoire d'un peuple*. Douarnenez: Ar Men, 1989.

Lavaud, René, and René Nelli, eds. and trans. *Flamenca*. In *Les troubadours*, 1:674–81. Paris: Desclée de Brouwer, 1960.

Leclercq, Jean. *L'amour des lettres et le désir de Dieu: Initiation aux auteurs monastiques du Moyen Age*. Paris, 1957.

Le Gentil, Pierre. *Le virelai et le villancico: Le problème des origines arabes*. Paris: Les Belles Lettres, 1954.

————. "La strophe zadjalesque, les khardjas et le problème des origines du lyrisme roman." *Romania* 84 (1963): 1–27, 209–50, 409–11.

Lévi-Strauss, Claude. *La pensée sauvage*. Paris: Plon, 1962.

————. *Structures élémentaires de la parenté*. Rev. and corrected ed. The Hague: Mouton, 1967.

————. *Regarder, écouter, lire*. Paris: Plon, 1993.

Limentani, Alberto. "Paléolgraphie, épopée et 'affaire Dreyfus.' Quelques remarques sur le thème: Paul Meyer et les chansons de geste." *Senefiance* 20–21 (1987): 815–42.

————. *Alle origini della filologia romanza*. Introduction by Mario Mancini. Parma: Pratiche Editrice, 1991.

Lorenzo Gradin, Pilar. *La cancion de mujer en la lirica medieval*. Santiago de Compostela: Universidade de Santiago de Compostela, 1990.

Lote, Georges. *Histoire du vers français. Première partie: le Moyen Age*. 3 vols. Paris: Hatier, 1949–55.

Marie de France. *The Lais of Marie de France*. Translated by Robert Hanning and Joan Ferrante. New York: E. P. Dutton, 1978.

————. *Lais*. Edited by Karl Warnke, translated by Laurence Harf-Lancner. Paris: Le Livre de Poche, "Lettres Gothiques," 1990.

Marot, Clément. *Oeuvres complètes*. Vol. 3, *Oeuvres lyriques*. Edited by C. A. Mayer. London: Athlone Press, 1964.

————. *Oeuvres poétiques*. Edited by Gérard Defaux. Paris: Classiques Garnier, 1993.

Mérimée, Prosper. *Lokis* (first publication in *Revue des Deux Mondes*, 15 September 1869, under the title *Le manuscrit du professeur Wittembach*). In *Romans et nouvelles*, edited by Henri Martineau, 716–75. Paris: Gallimard, Bibliothèque de la Pléiade, 1951.

Meyer, Rudolf Adelbert. *Französiche Lieder aus der Florentiner Hand-*

schrift Strozzi-Magliabecchiana. CL. VIII. 1040. Beihefte zur Zeitschrift für romanische Philologie 7. Halle: Niemeyer, 1907.

———. *Oeuvres poétiques.* Edited by Gérard Defaux. 2 vols. Paris: Classiques Garnier, 1990–93.

Molière. *Le misanthrope.* In *Oeuvres complètes,* vol. 2, edited by Georges Couton. Paris: Gallimard, Bibliothèque de la Pléiade, 1971.

Mölk, Ulrich. *Romanische Frauenlieder.* Munich: Wilhelm Fink, 1989.

Montaiglon, Anatole de, and Gaston Raynaud. *Recueil général des fabliaux,* vol. 1. Paris, 1872.

Montaigne, Michel de. *The Complete Works of Montaigne.* Translated by Donald M. Frame. Stanford: Stanford University Press, 1957.

Mortier, Roland. "Aspects du rêve chevaleresque de La Curne de Sainte-Palaye à Madame de Staël." In *Idéologie et propagande en France,* edited by Myriam Yardeni, 135–52. Paris: Picard, 1987.

Nagy, Gregory. *Pindar's Homer: The Lyric Possession of an Epic Past.* Baltimore: Johns Hopkins University Press, 1990.

Nerval, Gérard de. *Les vieilles ballades françaises (La Sylphide* of 10 July 1842), *Les Faux Saulniers* (1850), *Histoire de l'abbé de Bucquoy,* in *Les illuminés* (1852); *La Bohême galante* (1852), *Angélique,* and *Sylvie,* augmented by *Chansons et légendes du Valois,* in *Les filles du feu* (1854). In *Oeuvres complètes,* edited by Jean Guillaume and Claude Pichois. 3 vols. Paris: Gallimard, Bibliothèque de la Pléiade, 1984 (vol. 2), 1989 (vol. 1), 1993 (vol. 3).

Nietzsche, Friedrich. *On the Genealogy of Morals.* Translated by Walter Kaufmann. New York: Vintage, 1969.

———. *Untimely Meditations.* Translated by R. J. Hollingdale. New York: Cambridge University Press, 1983.

Novati, Francesco. *Gaston Paris.* In *A ricolta: Studi et profili.* Bergamo, 1907.

Olender, Maurice. *Les langues du paradis.* Paris: Le Seuil, 1994.

Panofsky, Erwin. *Gothic Architecture and Scholasticism.* New York: Meridian, 1957.

———. *Perspective as Symbolic Form.* Translated by Christopher S. Wood. New York: Zone, 1991.

Parducci, Amos. "La Canzone di 'mal maritata' in Francia nei secoli XV–XVI." *Romania* 38 (1909): 286–325.

Paris, Gaston. *Chansons du XVᵉ siècle publiées d'après le manuscrit de la Bibliothèque Nationale de Paris et accompagnées de la musique transcrite en notation moderne par Auguste Gevaërt.* Paris: SATF, 1875.

————. "De l'étude de la poésie populaire en France." *Mélusine* I (1878): 1–6.

————. *La poésie du moyen âge*. Paris, 1885.

————. "Les origines de la poésie lyrique en France au Moyen Age." *Journal des Savants* (1891): 674–88, 729–42; (1892): 155–67, 407–29. Reprinted in *Mélanges de Littérature du Moyen Age*, edited by Mario Roques, 539–613. Paris: Champion, 1912.

————. "Le cycle de la gageure." *Romania* 32 (1903): 481–551.

Paris, Paulin. *Discours d'ouverture, 1er mars 1853, Collège de France: Cours de langue et littérature françaises au Moyen Age*. Paris, 1853.

Pasero, Nicolo, ed. *Guiglielmo IX: Poesie*. Modena: S.T.E.M., 1973.

Pirot, François. *Recherches sur les connaissances littéraires des troubadours occitans et catalans des XIIe et XIIIe siècles*. Vol. 14, *Les "sirventès-ensen-hamens" de Guerau de Cabrera, Guiraut de Calanson et Bertrand de Paris*. Barcelona: Memorias de la Real Academia de Buenas Letras de Barcelona, 1972.

Poésies complètes du troubadour Marcabru. Edited by J.-M.-L. Dejeanne. Toulouse: E. Privat, 1909.

Poirion, Daniel. *Le poète et le prince: L'évolution du lyrisme courtois de Guillaume de Machaut à Charles d'Orléans*. Paris: PUF, 1965.

————. "Un document inédit: Note de P. Paris demandant la création d'une chaire de littérature du Moyen Age." *Perspectives Médiévales* 2 (November 1976): 4–5.

Pourrat, Henri. *Contes de la bûcheronne*. Paris: Alsatia, 1950.

Proust, Marcel. *Jean Santeuil*. Edition established by Pierre Clarac with the collaboration of Yves Sandre. Paris: Gallimard, Biliothèque de la Pléiade, 1971.

Quignard, Pascal. *La leçon de musique*. Paris: Hachette, 1987.

Renart, Jean. *Le roman de la Rose ou de Guillaume de Dole*. Edited by Félix Lecoy. Paris: Champion, CFMA, 1966.

————. *The Romance of the Rose or Guillaume de Dole*. Translated by Patricia Terry and Nancy Vine Durling. Phildelphia: University of Pennsylvania Press, 1993.

Roach, William, ed. *The Continuations of the Old French Perceval of Chrétien de Troyes*. Vol. 4, *The Second Continuation*. Philadelphia: American Philosophical Society, 1971.

Roncaglia, Aurelio. "Di una tradizione lirica pretrovadoresca in lingua volgare." *Cultura Neolatina* 11 (1951): 213–49.

Roquefort, B. de. *De l'état de la poésie française dans les XIIe et XIIIe* siècles. Edition of 1815, augmented with *Une dissertation sur la chanson, chez tous les peuples.* Paris: Audin and Pluquet, 1821.

Rousse, Michel. "Les chansons dans les farces." In *Musique, littérature et société*, Actes du colloque d'Amiens, edited by Danielle Buschinger. Paris: Champion, 1980.

Rousseau, Jean-Jacques. *La nouvelle Héloïse.* In *Oeuvres complètes*, vol. 2, edited by B. Guyon, J. Scherer, and C. Guyot. Paris: Gallimard, Bibliothèque de la Pléiade, 1961.

Sahr, Julius. *Das deutsche Volkslied.* Leipzig: Sammlung Göschen, 1901.

Sand, George. *Histoire de ma vie* (1854–55). In *Oeuvres autobiographiques*, vol. 1, edited by Georges Lubin. Paris: Gallimard, Bibliothèque de la Pléiade, 1970.

Spanke, Hans. *G. Raynauds Bibliographie des altfranzösischen Liedes.* Leiden: E. J. Brill, 1955.

Staël, Mme de. *De l'Allemagne.* Paris: Garnier-Flammarion, 1968.

Stanesco, Michel, and Michel Zink. *Histoire européenne du roman médiéval: Esquisses et perspectives.* Paris: PUF, 1992.

Tarbé, Prosper. *Romancero de Champagne.* 5 vols. Reims, 1863–64.

Tavera, Antoine. "Les chants du crépuscule à l'aube du *trobar*." In *Fin des temps et temps de la fin dans l'univers médiéval*, Senefiance 33: 495–517.

Tiersot, Julien. *Histoire de la chanson populaire en France.* Paris, 1889.

Tonnelat, Ernest. *Les contes des frères Grimm.* Paris, 1912.

Tresch, M. *Evolution de la chanson française savante et populaire.* Luxemburg, 1921.

Van den Boogaard, Nico H. J. *Rondeaux et refrains du XIIe au début du XIVe siècle.* Paris: Klincksieck, 1969.

Verrier, Paul. *Le vers français: Formes primitives—Développement—Diffusion.* 3 vols. Paris: Didier, 1931–32.

Vico, Jean-Baptiste. *Principes de la philosophie de l'histoire.* Translated from the *Scienza Nuova* and preceded by a discourse on the system and life of the author by Jules Michelet. Paris: Armand Colin, Bibliothèque de Cluny, 1963.

Villon, François. *The Ballads and Lyrics of François Villon.* Translated by John Payne, Dante Gabriel Rossetti, Algernon Charles Swinburne, Andrew Lang, and William Ernest Henley. Mount Vernon, N.Y.: Peter Pauper, 1940.

————. *Poésies complètes.* Edited by Claude Thiry. Paris: Le Livre de Poche, "Lettres Gothiques," 1991.

Wackernagel, Wilhelm. *Altfranzösische Lieder und Leiche aus Handschriften zu Berne und Beuenburg.* Basel, 1846.

Weckerlin, Jean-Baptiste. *La chanson populaire.* Paris: Firmin-Didot, 1887.

————. *L'ancienne chanson populaire en France (XVIᵉ et XVIIᵉ siècles).* Paris: Garnier, 1887.

Wolff, O. L. B. *Altfranzösische Lieder.* Leipzig, 1831.

Wolfzettel, Friedrich. "Französische Mediävistik im 19. Jahrhundert: Zur widersprüchlichen Aufwertung des Mittelalters." In *Mittelalter-Rezeption: Zur Rezeptionsgeschichte der romanischen Literaturen des Mittelalters in der Neuzeit,* edited by Reinhold Grimm, 181–96. Gegleitriehe zum GRLMA. Heidelberg: Carl Winter, 1991.

Zink, Michel. *La pastourelle: Poésie et folklore au Moyen Age.* Paris: Bordas, 1972.

————. *Les chansons de toile.* Paris: Champion, 1978.

————. *Roman rose et rose rouge: Le Roman de la Rose ou de Guillaume de Dole de Jean Renart.* Paris: Nizet, 1979.

————. *La subjectivité littéraire: Autour du siècle de saint Louis.* Paris: PUF, 1985.

————. "Lubias et Bélissant dans la chanson d'*Ami et Amile*." In *VIII Congresso de la Société Rencesvals, Pamplona—Santiago de Compestela, 15 a 25 de agosto de 1978,* 567–74. Pamplona, 1981. Reprinted in *Les voix de la conscience: Parole du poète et parole de Dieu au Moyen Age,* 101–14. Caen: Paradigme, 1992.

————. "Le lyrisme en rond: Esthétique et séduction des poèmes à forme fixe au Moyen Age." *Cahiers de l'Association Internationale des Etudes Françaises* 32 (1980): 71–90. Reprinted in *Les voix de la conscience,* 177–96.

————. "La suffisance du paysan dans la littérature française du Moyen Age." In *Der Bauer im Wandel der Zeit,* edited by Willi Hirdt. Bonn: Bouvier Verlag, 1986. Reprinted in *Les voix de la conscience,* 247–60.

————. *Les voix de la conscience: Parole du poète et parole de Dieu au Moyen Age.* Caen: Paradigme, 1992.

Zumthor, Paul. *Langue, texte, énigme.* Paris: Le Seuil, 1957.

————. *Langue et technique poétique à l'époque romane (XIᵉ–XIIIᵉ siècles).* Paris: Klincksieck, 1963.

―――. *Essai de poétique médiévale.* Paris: Le Seuil, 1972.

―――. *Le masque et la lumière: La poétique des grands rhétoriqueurs.* Paris: Le Seuil, 1978.

―――. *Introduction à la poésie orale.* Paris: Le Seuil, 1983.

―――. *La lettre et la voix: De la "littérature" médiévale.* Paris: Le Seuil, 1987.

Library of Congress Cataloging-in-Publication Data

Zink, Michel.
    [Moyen Age et ses chansons. English]
    The enchantment of the Middle Ages / by Michel Zink ; translated
by Jane Marie Todd.
        p.   cm. — (Parallax: re-visions of culture and society)
    Includes bibliographical references and index.
    ISBN 0-8018-5818-6 (alk. paper)
        1. French poetry—To 1500—History and criticism.
2. Civilization, Medieval, in literature.   I. Title.   II. Series :
Parallax (Baltimore, Md.)
PQ 151.Z5413 1998
841'.109—dc21   97-35521
                                                              CIP